RAND NATIONAL DEFENSE RESEARCH INSTITUTE

America's Pacific Island Allies

The Freely Associated States and Chinese Influence

Derek Grossman, Michael S. Chase, Gerard Finin,
Wallace Gregson, Jeffrey W. Hornung, Logan Ma,
Jordan R. Reimer, Alice Shih

Prepared for the Office of the Secretary of Defense

For more information on this publication, visit www.rand.org/t/RR2973

Library of Congress Cataloging-in-Publication Data is available for this publication.
ISBN: 978-1-9774-0228-8

Cover photo: Palau islands by Adobe Stock / BlueOrange Studio.

Support RAND
Make a tax-deductible charitable contribution at
www.rand.org/giving/contribute

www.rand.org

Preface

Located north and northeast of Australia and east of the Philippines, the Freely Associated States (FAS)—comprising the independent countries of the Republic of Palau, the Federated States of Micronesia (FSM), and the Republic of the Marshall Islands (RMI)—occupy an ocean area roughly the size of the continental United States. Their location contains sea lines of communication linking U.S. military forces to Australia and Guam, and Guam to the Philippines. These strategic advantages have made the region particularly attractive to China, which has recently been attempting to expand its influence in this area—a development that could have significant implications for U.S. national interests in the region.

The purpose of this report is to explain the importance of the FAS in U.S. defense and foreign policy, describe China's growing influence in the FAS, analyze how other countries in the region are responding, and assess the implications for the United States. This research was undertaken in response to the National Defense Authorization Act (NDAA) passed in 2018. The NDAA called for an independent entity to conduct an unclassified study examining U.S. defense and foreign policy interests and Chinese influence in the FAS. As an independent report, the study does not represent the views of the U.S. government.

This research was sponsored by the Office of the Secretary of Defense and conducted within the International Security and Defense Policy Center of the RAND National Defense Research Institute (NDRI), a federally funded research and development center (FFRDC) sponsored by the Office of the Secretary of Defense, the Joint Staff, the Unified Combatant Commands, the Navy, the Marine Corps, the defense agencies, and the defense Intelligence Community.

For more information on the International Security and Defense Policy Center, see www.rand.org/nsrd/ndri/centers/isdp or contact the director (contact information is provided on the webpage).

Contents

Figures and Table

Figures

Table

Summary

The Freely Associated States (FAS)—comprising the Republic of Palau, the Federated States of Micronesia (FSM), and the Republic of the Marshall Islands (RMI)—collectively cover a wide expanse in the North Pacific roughly the size of the continental United States. Despite having small populations and limited natural resources, these three sovereign states are crucial to the promotion of Washington's Indo-Pacific Strategy. The unique agreements governing U.S. relations with the FAS—known as "Compacts of Free Association"—offer the U.S. military exclusive and secure access to the land, sea, and air routes of this enormous region. In short, the FAS are tantamount to a power-projection superhighway running through the heart of the North Pacific into Asia. It effectively connects U.S. military forces in Hawaii to those in theater, particularly to forward operating positions on the U.S. territory of Guam.

The expansion of China's engagement in the FAS raises important questions about the fate of this geostrategically vital region. The Pacific Islands are part of China's 21st Century Maritime Silk Road. We assess that China, through its Pacific Island engagements, seeks to more fully incorporate the region into its signature Belt and Road Initiative (BRI). Beijing supports such an approach by boosting investment and economic assistance to the islands. China's heightened role in the Pacific is also designed to further reduce the number of diplomatic partners recognizing Taiwan. Out of Taipei's 17 remaining allies, six are in the Pacific, and two are in the FAS (Palau and the RMI). Finally, publications by Chinese scholars suggest that Beijing views the region as strategically important in the context of competition with the United States.

This report examines the importance of the FAS to U.S. defense and foreign policy interests, assesses the extent to which China is making inroads into the FAS, evaluates the responses of other countries in the FAS, and analyzes the implications for U.S. interests. This research was undertaken in response to the National Defense Authorization Act (NDAA) of fiscal year 2018. The NDAA called for an independent entity to conduct an unclassified study examining U.S. defense and foreign policy interests and Chinese influence in the FAS. As an independent report, this study does not represent the views of the U.S. Department of Defense or the United States government.

Characteristics of the Compacts of Free Association

The Compacts of Free Association (referred to as Compacts) are unique international agreements governing the bilateral relationships between the United States and the FAS. The Compacts enable the parties to maintain close and mutually beneficial ties. After gaining independence, the FSM, the RMI, and Palau joined the United Nations (UN) and other international institutions with full membership rights and responsibilities. At the same time, the Compacts provided for continued U.S. economic assistance and exclusive U.S. military access. Under the Compacts, the U.S. Department of the Interior's Office of Insular Affairs (OIA) retains overall fiscal management responsibility for U.S. assistance to the FAS, while the Department of State handles government-to-government relations. Many other U.S. agencies provide services to these island nations. Key provisions within the Compacts fall into the three categories of government relations, economic relations, and security and defense relations.

Each individual Compact of Free Association (COFA) establishes its respective country as a self-governing nation with the capacity to conduct its own foreign affairs, in consultation with the United States, including the right to enter into treaties and other international agreements with foreign governments, regional organizations, and international organizations. The Compacts also provide FAS citizens with certain immigration privileges, such as the right to live, work, and study in the United States indefinitely, as well as the right to enter the United States without a visa (with reciprocal benefits for U.S. citizens entering both the FSM and the RMI).

The Compacts also allow the FAS to receive economic assistance from the United States. Economic assistance has primarily taken the form of grants and contributions to Compact Trust Funds (individual trust funds set up for the countries of the FAS), federal services, as well as discretionary spending by federal agencies. For the FAS, economic assistance supports a variety of sectors, but tends to prioritize healthcare, education, and infrastructure. The permanent appropriation that enables direct grant-based economic assistance to the FAS could cease at the end of fiscal year (FY) 2023 for the FSM and the RMI, and at the end of FY2024 for Palau, if new agreements are not reached between Washington and the FAS, whereupon disbursements from Compact Trust Funds will provide a source of income to each respective Freely Associated State. However, the termination of Compact-related grant assistance, and the shift to Compact Trust Fund disbursements from FY 2024 onwards, is a matter of controversy. Multiple analyses indicate that trust-fund disbursements will not make up for the budget shortfall expected when grant-based assistance terminates.

The Compacts allow the United States and the FAS to maintain a mutually beneficial relationship, particularly the security and defense relationship, as none of the FAS have indigenous militaries. The Compacts allow the United States to maintain sole and unfettered military access to the lands, waterways, and airspace of the FAS. The Compacts include provisions for indefinite U.S. authority for defense and security matters, denial of access to the area to potential adversaries, U.S. defense sites and operating rights, and service in the U.S. armed forces for FAS citizens. Taken together, the security and defense provisions of the Compacts form an essential foundation for U.S. national security interests in the region. In particular, as a consequence of these security and defense provisions, the Compacts deny an enormous and strategically important section of the Western Pacific to potential U.S. adversaries, while enabling U.S. presence and power projection in the region.

China's Geostrategic Outlook on the Pacific

In comparison to other areas of geostrategic importance, such as the South China Sea, there is little publicly available Chinese analysis focusing specifically on the FAS. Nevertheless, Chinese analysts increasingly view the Pacific region more broadly as closely tied to China's national security interests. The region's strategic location astride major maritime passageways, abundance in certain natural resources, and political power as a voting bloc in international organizations lend it growing value in Chinese foreign policy, particularly as China's overseas interests and influence expand. That statements from the highest levels of the Chinese foreign-policy apparatus characterize the Pacific as a natural fit for extending the maritime components of Beijing's BRI suggest the high importance accorded to the region.

Chinese analysts identify two types of security threats that are prominent in the Pacific Islands region. The first entails such nontraditional threats as political instability, piracy, terrorism, transnational crime, and natural disasters. As the world's second-largest economy and largest trading nation, nontraditional security threats could have an adverse impact on China's economic development. The second type of threat is the potential geostrategic encirclement by the United States and its allies. As part of the "Second Island Chain" (a line of islands from the Kurils down to the Marianas and including Guam), Chinese observers have noted that these islands form a natural barrier to China's maritime expansion into the open ocean.

At least one Chinese observer has alluded to the possibility of a long-term military presence in the region, arguing for the establishment of so-called "strategic fulcrum ports" in the Pacific to secure maritime access in the region. These ports could provide China's People's Liberation Army Navy (PLAN) with supply points that would be conducive to reducing the gap in hard power between China and the United States. Beijing has also focused on gaining traction in the region through expanding its influence, primarily through diplomatic and economic engagement.

China's Influence in the Freely Associated States

Pacific island nations have witnessed China's rise, and Beijing has made significant strides as a major trade, aid, investment, and diplomatic partner for a number of countries in the region. Chinese companies are increasingly active across the entire region in a broad range of commercial ventures. China's desire to erode Taiwan's international space is a key driver of its activities in the Pacific. However, China has expanded its focus to one of broader influence—not just on competition with Taiwan for recognition—a trend that is reflected by its relations with each of the FAS.

China's Relationship with the Federated States of Micronesia

The FSM established formal diplomatic relations with China in 1989. Since that time, the relationship has grown, including the 2014 creation of the commission on economic trade cooperation. China's economic relationship with FSM includes substantial trade and aid components. More recently, the FSM has signed a memorandum of understanding with China to join Beijing's BRI. Chinese embassy discretionary grants occasionally provide much-needed heavy equipment on an ad-hoc basis. Larger infrastructure projects have ranged from building official residences for government officials at the national and state levels, to providing ships for inter-island transport. The most ambitious Chinese investment proposal in FSM, to date, has been the plan to build a 10,000-room holiday resort and casino complex in the state of Yap, and to establish direct airline connections to facilitate ease of travel for vacationers. The Chinese also proposed building a 200-room hotel with a casino in Pohnpei, a project which is currently being backed by the Pohnpei Governor and considered by the Pohnpei legislature.

Chinese contacts with state governments and state officials are also numerous. In August 2017, for example, Chinese Vice Minister of Foreign Affairs Zheng Zeguang visited Pohnpei with a high-level delegation and met with FSM political leaders. President Peter Christian of FSM was also accorded a state visit to Beijing in March 2017—an honor that has had a lasting positive effect on FSM's perception of China. A key topic of the dialogues between the two countries is the

U.S. Compact Trust Fund that the government of the FSM will rely on if U.S. economic assistance expires in 2023. Beijing has suggested that China might be willing to supplement the Compact Trust Fund to help the FSM achieve greater self-reliance.

Chuuk State, the FSM's largest state, has expressed interest in becoming a sovereign nation; this could emerge as an important consideration in the context of China's relationship with the FSM. Throughout the FSM's history there has been domestic internal contention between the state and the national government over the equitable distribution of non–COFA funding (fisheries and tax revenue). The United States has consistently maintained that its relationship is with the national government in Palikir, and any movement by a state to secede would, if a state were no longer part of the federation, presumably mean an end to the COFA in all its dimensions. While this understanding has implicitly buttressed national unity, the cessation of economic support after FY 2023 may undermine national cohesion. Such a development could have important strategic implications. The Chuuk lagoon, one of the Pacific's largest and deepest, was once a critically important location for the Japanese Navy, and remains a potentially important strategic naval asset.

China's Relationship with the Republic of the Marshall Islands

Although it does not receive diplomatic recognition from the RMI, Beijing nevertheless has a number of channels that could allow it to exercise influence there. Trade is an important part of China's relationship with the RMI, even though the RMI still maintains official diplomatic relations with Taiwan. In particular, China maintains commercial ties to the island through fishing companies such as Pan Pacific Foods. In the absence of official diplomatic recognition of China, it appears that the head of Pan Pacific Foods is considered an unofficial Chinese representative to the RMI. Beijing is also a part owner in the Marshall Islands Fishing Company, a major enterprise in the RMI, and Chinese businessmen own small stores in the RMI.

At the Asia World Expo, held in Hong Kong in April 2018, a Chinese businessman and the Mayor of Rongelap Atoll proposed the creation of a special administrative region to attract investment to the atoll and Beijing may be trying to set up an administrative region there. The proposal quickly became a source of controversy in RMI politics, stemming from concerns that it could create a haven for money laundering and other illegal activities. The government declined to back the proposal after it was declared unconstitutional by the RMI Attorney General. Rongelap is located near the Ronald Reagan Ballistic Missile Defense Test Site at Kwajalein Atoll—potentially raising concerns for U.S. policymakers about Chinese spying on the facility.

In addition, China is imposing extra taxes on RMI-flagged ships entering its ports. This is a particularly vulnerable pressure point for the RMI, as its flag is the third-most-common registered flag on international commercial ships. Beijing is also offering the prospect of an influx of financial assistance via the BRI to try to convince the government of the RMI to formally switch recognition from Taipei to Beijing, according to interviewees.

China's Relationship with Palau

Trade is an important component of China's relationship with Palau, even though Palau maintains official diplomatic relations with Taiwan rather than China. Beijing also appears to be trying to use tourism to advance its objectives in Palau. Chinese tour agents are promoting group package tours there via commercial and charter flights, and these tour groups have rapidly come to constitute the largest share of Palau's tourism industry. Between 2011 and 2015, the number of Chinese tourists soared to more than 50 percent of annual visitor arrivals—until November 2017, when Beijing apparently decided to precipitously drop the numbers, hurting Palau's economy. China's objective is almost certainly to persuade Palau to switch diplomatic relations. Although Taiwan has increased its support for Palau's tourism industry, its ability to offset the loss of Chinese visitors is likely limited.

Activities of Other Countries in Oceania and the Freely Associated States

A number of other countries have interests in Oceania more broadly and in the FAS. China's rising profile within the broader region and in the FAS specifically has prompted responses by other actors, including Australia, New Zealand, Taiwan, and Japan.

Australia

Australia's engagement in the broader Pacific region has already become more intense as China has bolstered its presence. Senior officials have stated that China's construction of roads, ports, airports, and other infrastructure in the broader region has triggered concern in Canberra that small Pacific nations may be saddled with unsustainable debts from China. However, Australia has traditionally focused more heavily on other parts of the region, and Australia's footprint in the FAS is modest compared to its engagement in the broader region. Its sole ambassador in the FAS, based in the FSM, has multiple accreditations: to the FSM, the RMI, and Palau, and (as Consul General) to Guam and the Commonwealth of the Northern Mariana Islands. Canberra recognizes that as the strategic environment in the FAS becomes more competitive, it will have to increase its involvement in the area accordingly. As such, Australia is planning on opening diplomatic posts in both Palau and the RMI by 2020. Notably, in June 2014, Canberra unveiled its $1.88 billion Pacific Patrol Boat Program, which included all of the FAS, giving it additional leverage in the regional security domain.

New Zealand

Like Australia, New Zealand has focused much more heavily on the South Pacific, but Wellington also has active relationships with the FAS. The New Zealand Consulate General in Honolulu, Hawaii, is also accredited to Palau, the RMI, and the FSM. New Zealand's bilateral ties with the FAS are centered on such common interests as security, fisheries management, development, climate change, and regional trade. However, Wellington is concerned about increasing strategic rivalry between the United States and China and growing Chinese influence. As part of its "Pacific Reset" policy for the broader region, New Zealand has pledged to strengthen its engagement with the FAS, including by increasing its overseas development funding and encouraging stepped-up U.S. activities in Oceania.

Taiwan

Oceania is one of several arenas of diplomatic competition between Beijing and Taipei. Over the past two years, Beijing has succeeded in establishing links with five of Taipei's previous diplomatic allies, leaving Taipei with only 17 states recognizing Taiwan instead of China. Six of these remaining allies are in the Pacific, and two of them are FAS—the RMI and Palau both recognize Taipei. As such, Taiwan prioritizes maintaining its ties with the RMI and Palau, and it remains actively engaged with both countries diplomatically and economically.

Japan

Since its pre–World War II colonialization of the islands that eventually became the FAS, Japan has maintained close ties with these islands and continues to have a strong interest in them and other Pacific islands. Japan has focused on issues important to the Pacific islands, such as climate change adaptation strategies, building resilience to natural disasters, and strengthening states' capabilities to enforce the rule of law. Japan is also heavily engaged with each Freely Associated State and maintains embassies in the FSM, the RMI, and Palau. Moving forward, Japan hopes to expand its engagement with the FAS in a number of areas, including maritime security training and resources.

Implications

Although primarily aimed at the broader Indo-Pacific region, Washington's "free and open Indo-Pacific" strategy also equally applies to securing the FAS. History underscores that the FAS play a vital role in U.S. defense strategy. As demonstrated by Imperial Japan's actions during World War II, the location of the FAS and expansive geographic sprawl can clearly be a significant advantage if properly leveraged. If ignored or subverted, they could become, as in the past, a critical vulnerability. The U.S. National Security Strategy (NSS) supports keeping these large areas of ocean "free and open" and calls for sustaining favorable balances of power through strong commitment and close cooperation with allies and partners.

China's engagement in the FAS highlights the importance it attaches to this part of the Pacific. Beijing likely believes the FAS are critical strategic locations for U.S. power projection into Asia. Therefore, China is likely to seek ways to challenge American dominance there by floating economic incentives to the FAS in exchange for loosened ties to Washington. This will increasingly be the case if U.S.-China relations continue down a competitive and adversarial path. Regardless, Beijing views the FAS as relevant to the pursuit of its economic goals, especially through the BRI, and also relevant to its efforts to persuade Taiwan's remaining diplomatic partners to switch recognition to the mainland.

Going forward, the United States, its allies, and its partners should demonstrate their commitment to the region by maintaining appropriate levels of funding to the FAS, and strengthening engagement with the FAS more broadly. Failure to do so would be a self-inflicted wound that could come at the expense of the foreign policy and defense interests of the United States and its allies and partners. This will become particularly relevant after the current economic support arrangements between Washington and the FSM and the RMI expire after FY 2023 (Palau after FY 2024). To a greater extent than at any time since gaining independence, the FAS are vulnerable to accepting alternative sources of revenue, which China will likely provide as part of a strategy aimed at improving its position in the region. Therefore, this should serve as a catalyst for the opening of a productive new chapter in how the United States and its allies and partners engage with the FAS.

Acknowledgments

The authors wish to express their appreciation to the numerous scholars, analysts, and officials, as well as other individuals, who offered their expertise on the FAS and the Compacts of Free Association, the activities of China and other countries in the region, and a number of related issues. We would also like to thank Christine Wormuth, Lyle Morris, and Robert Scher for their reviews of the draft report.

Abbreviations

BRI   Belt & Road Initiative

CASS   Chinese Academy of Social Sciences

CIIS   China Institute of International Studies

COFA   Compact of Free Association

EEZ   exclusive economic zone

FAS   Freely Associated States

FSM   Federated States of Micronesia

GAO   Government Accountability Office

IMF   International Monetary Fund

MUORA   Military Use and Operating Rights Agreement

NDAA   National Defense Authorization Act

NSS   National Security Strategy

ODA   official development assistance

PIF   Pacific Islands Forum

PALM   Pacific Islands Leaders Meeting

PLA   People's Liberation Army

PLAN   People's Liberation Army Navy
RMI   Republic of the Marshall Islands
TTPI   Trust Territory of the Pacific Islands
USAKA   U.S. Army Kwajalein Atoll
UN   United Nations

CHAPTER ONE

Introduction

Located to the north and northeast of Australia and east of the Philippines, the Freely Associated States (FAS)—the Republic of Palau, the Federated States of Micronesia (FSM), and the Republic of the Marshall Islands (RMI)—collectively cover a wide expanse of some 3,473,751 square miles in the North Pacific, or roughly the size of the continental United States (see Figure 1.1).[1]

Despite having small populations and limited natural resources, these three sovereign states are crucial to the promotion of Washington's Indo-Pacific Strategy. The unique partnerships governing U.S. relations with the FAS—formalized by each Freely Associated State as a Compact of Free Association (COFA) with the United States—offer the U.S. military exclusive access to the land, sea, and air routes of this enormous region.

In short, the FAS are tantamount to a power-projection superhighway running through the heart of the North Pacific into Asia, connecting U.S. military forces in Hawaii to those in theater, particularly to forward-operating positions on the U.S. territory of Guam. Indeed, the FAS (at the time part of the Japanese mandate) were critical to the U.S. island-hopping campaign that led to victory over Imperial Japan in World War II. Since then, however, the region has largely been taken for granted, even as it continues to offer secure sea lines

---

[1] The FAS are located in the North Pacific, as opposed to the South Pacific (below the equator), which is home to such other Pacific island countries as Fiji, Niue, Tonga, Vanuatu, and others. The terms "Oceania," "Pacific," or "Pacific Island region" will be used here to describe the residents of both the North and South Pacific regions.

Figure 1.1
Map of the Freely Associated States

SOURCE: Provided to the RAND Corporation by the U.S. Department of State.

of communication and a potential staging ground for emergencies or military contingencies in Asia. In large part, this is due to the lack of competition for influence in the FAS—that is, until recently.

The expansion of China's engagement in the FAS raises important questions about the fate of this geostrategically vital region. According to a recent report by the U.S.-China Economic and Security Review Commission, Beijing's growing influence in the region "could threaten Compact of Free Association agreements . . . over the long term."[2] More

---

[2]   Ethan Meick, Michelle Ker, and Chan Han May, "China's Engagement in the Pacific Islands: Implications for the United States," U.S.-China Economic and Security Review

broadly, the Commission argues that China, through Pacific Island engagements, seeks to incorporate the region into its signature Belt and Road Initiative (BRI) to gain access to raw materials and natural resources. Beijing is doing this by boosting economic assistance to the islands.

China's heightened role in the Pacific is also designed to further reduce the number of diplomatic partners recognizing Taiwan. Out of Taipei's 17 remaining allies, six are in the Pacific, and two are part of the FAS (Palau and the RMI). Finally, our analysis of Chinese articles and commentary on Beijing's objectives in the Pacific concludes that China likely views the region as increasingly important from a security perspective as well.

Objective and Organization of This Report

The purpose of this report is to (1) examine the importance of the FAS to U.S. defense and foreign policy interests, (2) assess the extent to which China is making inroads into the FAS, (3) evaluate the activities and responses of other countries in the FAS and broader Oceania, and (4) analyze the implications for U.S. defense and foreign policy interests. This research was undertaken in response to the National Defense Authorization Act (NDAA) for fiscal year 2018. The NDAA called for an independent entity to conduct an unclassified study examining U.S. defense and foreign policy interests and Chinese influence in the FAS. As an independent report, the study does not represent the views of the United States government.

Chapter Two presents a snapshot of each Freely Associated State and explains how the FAS first came into existence. It further offers a primer on the Compacts themselves, as these agreements are extremely unique and thus poorly understood, even by seasoned foreign policy

---

Commission, June 14, 2018. For additional literature on China's overall approach to the Pacific, see, for example, Anne-Marie Brady, "China's Foreign Influence Offensive in the Pacific," *War on the Rocks*, September 29, 2017; and Joanne Wallis, "Is China Changing the 'Rules' in the Pacific Islands?" *The Strategist*, Australian Strategic Policy Institute, April 11, 2018.

professionals. Chapter Three evaluates the extent to which Beijing has made economic, diplomatic, and military inroads into the FAS. Chapter Four analyzes the activities of other countries in the Pacific (potentially in response to China's rising role there), including Taiwan, Japan, Australia, and New Zealand. Finally, Chapter Five offers concluding thoughts and implications for U.S. defense and foreign policy interests in the FAS and for the broader Pacific region.

A Note on Sources

Three main sources of information shaped development of this report. First, we analyzed open-source primary source publications to gauge Chinese views of the importance of the FAS and Oceania more generally. Second, we reviewed official and unofficial publications, academic literature, think-tank commentary, journal articles, and other sources to develop context for Chinese activities in the FAS. Finally, we interviewed a number of interlocutors, including U.S. and foreign government officials, academics, and think tank experts to supplement our findings. Our assessments are based on the repeated emergence of several key themes across multiple sources.

CHAPTER TWO

The Freely Associated States and Compacts of Free Association

This chapter offers snapshots of each FAS country. It then describes the history of how the FAS came into existence, and their roles, through the Compacts, of promoting U.S. foreign policy and defense interests, including U.S. defense posture and plans.

What Are the Freely Associated States?

Each Freely Associated State has its own distinctive history, culture, political system, and economic trajectory. Despite the obvious asymmetries between the interactions of a continental power and smaller island states, the basic U.S. relationships with the three Freely Associated States have been marked by mutual respect for sovereignty that has, in turn, advanced the national interests of each country (described in detail further in this chapter). Over the past three decades, there has never been serious consideration by any of the parties to withdraw from the Compacts.

The FAS are viewed internationally as peaceful, stable democracies that regularly hold free and fair elections and maintain commendable human rights records. Within the United Nations (UN), the voting records of the FSM, the RMI, and Palau are ranked as being among the most consistent with positions taken by the United States. Under the Compacts, U.S. financial assistance is vital to the FAS, and citizens of these countries value the ability to enter the United States

5

without a visa to study, work, or reside without limitations. The defense provisions of the compacts have meant that the FAS have not needed to provide for national defense. Qualified citizens of the FAS are eligible to join the U.S. military, and increasing numbers have served in all branches of the armed forces stationed around the globe.

Federated States of Micronesia

Among the FAS, the FSM is by far the most populous, with an estimated 103,643 citizens.[1] A central challenge is the creation of a shared national vision among its four culturally diverse states: Chuuk, Kosrae, Pohnpei, and Yap. With primary and secondary educational systems that struggle to achieve adequate quality, the FSM remains committed to development of local capacity. Unlike its neighbors, the FSM has limited the number of migrants it accepts, to emphasize self-reliance— even if this has meant lower rates of economic growth.

Palikir, the capital, seeks to become a northern Pacific headquarters for regional organizations to bring in new opportunities for business development. The increasing importance of Guam as a site for U.S. military personnel may offer prospects for tourism in nearby Chuuk, Yap, and Pohnpei. The more conservative pace of change being pursued by the FSM, through investments in its own citizens' human capital, may over the longer term offer enhanced development prospects.[2]

At the same time, out-migration to the United States has grown. Survey data suggests that one out of every three FSM citizens—about 50,000 people—reside in the United States. The FSM's out-migration rates to the United States suggest many Micronesians realize the benefits of access to employment in a larger economy, or wish to avail themselves of educational opportunities. Although the most popular destinations in the early years of nationhood favored Guam and Hawaii, today increasing numbers of Micronesians are establishing residence in the continental United States. It is estimated that in every year from 2000 to 2012, some 1,200 FSM citizens moved to the continental

---

[1]   Central Intelligence Agency, *World Factbook*, Washington, D.C., 2016.

[2]   Gerard A. Finin, "Envisioning the North Pacific Economies Post 2023," *ADB Pacific Economic Monitor: Midyear Review*, July 2013.

United States to find jobs, take advantage of the reduced cost of living, and escape some of the negative stereotypes of Micronesians found in Hawaii and Guam.[3] From the perspective of many FSM citizens, the right to reside in the United States is by far the most important feature of the free association agreement.

Republic of the Marshall Islands

The strategic value of the RMI (population 53,000) to the United States arguably exceeds that of the other two FAS. From both the historical and contemporary perspectives, the relationship between the RMI and the United States is complex. Overall economic support from the United States to the RMI, from 2004 to 2023, is estimated to total $1.5 billion.[4] Washington is committed to paying at least $18 million per year (2017 was $21 million, adjusted for inflation) in Compact funding to the RMI government through 2066, for exclusive long-term use of Kwajalein Atoll as a U.S. base (the Ronald Reagan Ballistic Missile Defense Test Site).[5]

For over five decades the RMI's Kwajalein Atoll has remained a strategic location for the U.S. Department of Defense. The U.S. Army Kwajalein Atoll (USAKA) hosts several critical defense-related activities on Kwajalein. The largest tenant is the Ronald Reagan Ballistic Missile Defense Test Site, which provides the United States with a unique ability to test intercontinental ballistic missiles, ballistic missile defense, and hypersonics, as well as an ample spectrum required for space surveillance, space object identification, and monitoring new foreign launches. Kwajalein also hosts the U.S. Air Force's Space Fence program, designed to detect and track space debris threatening satel-

---

[3] Hezel, Francis, *Micronesians on the Move: Eastward and Upward Bound*, Honolulu, Hawaii: East-West Center, 2013.

[4] For the $1.5 billion figure, see David B. Gootnick, *Compact of Free Association: Implementation Activities Have Progressed, but the Marshall Islands Faces Challenges to Achieving Long-Term Compact Goals*, U.S. Government Accountability Office, Washington, D.C., July 25, 2007.

[5] Regarding U.S. payments, see David B. Gootnick, *Compacts of Free Association: Actions Needed for the Transition of Micronesia and the Marshall Islands to Trust Fund Income*, U.S. Government Accountability Office, Washington, D.C., May 2018.

lites when it achieves initial operating capability in mid-2019.[6] Over
the past decade, facility investments apparently in excess of $1 billion
are indicative of both the importance of the base and the long-range
U.S. plans for its use.[7] Current land-use rent agreements have options
for renewal through 2086.[8] There is no other similar type of facility in
the FAS. The only other defense-related activity across the FAS is in
Palau, where the United States is working to install a radar facility on
the island.[9]

In addition, the United States has paid approximately $600 mil-
lion in compensation (over $1 billion in current dollars) and remedia-
tion for nuclear testing that occurred in the RMI between 1946 and
1958;[10] the U.S. nuclear weapons testing program detonated 67 nuclear
weapons between 1946 and 1958. In 1987, Congress appropriated $150
million to the RMI as a final settlement for nuclear radiation–related
claims. Bikini Atoll residents received $75 million over 15 years, and
the remainder was allocated to trust funds. In 1992, an additional $90
million was conveyed for the resettlement trust fund. By some estimates, Washington provides nearly 80 percent of the RMI's annual
budget.[11]

As is true of citizens of the FSM and Palau, the Marshall Islands
have benefitted from visa-free entry to the United States. It is estimated
that about 1,000 Marshall Islanders emigrate to the United States each

---

6   Wyatt Olson, "Space Fence on Kwajalein Atoll Will Allow Air Force to Monitor Debris,
Threats," *Stars and Stripes*, April 10, 2017.

7   The $1 billion figure is based on an interview with Norman Barth, Deputy Chief of Mis-
sion, United States Embassy, Republic of the Marshall Islands, August 4, 2015.

8   For options to renew the rental agreement out to 2086, see Gootnick, 2018.

9   Wyatt Olson, "U.S. to Install Radar Systems on Tiny Pacific Island Nation of Palau,"
Stars and Stripes, August 28, 2017.

10   U.S. Embassy in the Marshall Islands, "The Legacy of U.S. Nuclear Testing and Radiation Exposure in the Marshall Islands," webpage, September 15, 2012.

11   Thomas Lum and Bruce Vaughn, *The Pacific Islands: Policy Issues*, Washington, D.C.:
Congressional Research Service, Report 7-5700, February 2017.

year.[12] In 2016 alone, nearly 10,000 Marshall Islanders entered the United States, although many presumably returned home.[13] A special U.S. Census Bureau survey in 2001 indicated that there were as many as 6,000 Marshallese in Springdale, Arkansas, a number that may be much larger today. The Marshallese migration to this industrial city is said to have made it host to the largest population of Marshall Islanders outside of RMI,[14] and the RMI has opened a consulate in the area.[15] In 2017, remittance flows to the RMI totaled $28 million.[16] All of these interactions with the United States underscore the importance of the related provisions of COFA to the RMI.

As an increasing number of Marshall Islanders leave for employment in the United States, the 2011 Census of the Marshall Islands documented an increase in international migration to the Marshall Islands. Between 2006 and 2011, 1,434 individuals entered as migrants, with 80 percent residing in the capital of Majuro. An estimated 43 percent were from the United States, while only 9.6 percent were from China.[17] Some of the increase in flows from the United States may be attributable to children born in the United States to Marshall Islander parents who have returned home.[18]

---

[12] Francis Hezel, *Is That the Best You Can Do? A Tale of Two Micronesian Economies*, Honolulu, Hawaii: East-West Center, 2006, p. 31.

[13] U.S. Department of State, "U.S. Relations with Marshall Islands," July 5, 2018.

[14] Christopher Leonard, "In the Remote Marshall Islands, Residents Dream and Save for Years for a New Life in Arkansas," *Arkansas Democrat Gazette*, January 10, 2005.

[15] Bret Schulte, "For Pacific Islanders, Hopes and Troubles in Arkansas," *New York Times*, July 4, 2012.

[16] "Migration and Remittances Data," World Bank, November 16, 2017; Francis X. Hezel, *Pacific Island Nations: How Viable Are Their Economies?* Honolulu, Hawaii: East-West Center, 2012.

[17] Secretariat of the Pacific Community, *Republic of the Marshall Islands 2011 Census Report*, Noumea, New Caledonia, 2012.

[18] Secretariat of the Pacific Community, 2012, pp. 34–35.

Palau

Palau has developed one of the most successful private-sector economies in the Pacific. With the smallest population of any FAS country (approximately 22,000), Palau's pristine natural environment and
favorable location for East Asian visitors has been used to its advantage
in building a dynamic tourism industry. Today tourism accounts for
42.3 percent of Palau's gross domestic product (GDP). By numerous
measures, it is among the most prosperous of the Pacific island nations,
with a gross national income per capita of approximately $13,000.[19]
Palau's success as an international tourist destination has made it the
most highly globalized North Pacific nation. It was ranked 60 out of
186 countries on the 2017 Human Development Index, the highest
of any developing country in the Pacific.[20] In contrast, the FSM was
ranked 131, and the RMI was ranked 106. At the same time, however,
Palau's tourism industry is vulnerable on two fronts: heavy reliance
on tourists coming from a single country, and dependence on foreign
labor in the private sector.

Palau has bilateral relations with more than 40 countries and
entities, including the United States, Japan, Israel, and the European
Union. Like the RMI, Palau also has diplomatic relations with Taiwan
that were formally established in 1999. The evolution of Palau's foreign
policy began in the early 1990s. Prior to independence, in 1994, policymakers accepted invitations from China and Taiwan for informal
talks. Decisions regarding Palau's bilateral relationships were considered, and the talks included extensive internal debate. In 1997, Palau's
first president following full independence, Kuniwo Nakamura, was
invited to visit both countries. After a more than a year, the executive
branch made its decision, and Taiwan opened its embassy in the old
capital of Koror.[21]

---

19 Francis X. Hezel, *On Your Mark, Get Set…Tourism's Take-Off in Micronesia*, Honolulu,
Hawaii: East-West Center, 2017.

20 United Nations, *2017 Human Development Index*, New York: United Nations, 2018.

21 Takashi Mita, "Changing Attitudes and the Two Chinas in the Republic of Palau," in T.
Wesley Smith and Edward Porter (eds.), *China in Oceania: Reshaping the Pacific?* New York:
Berghahn Books, 2010, pp. 180–181.

Since that time, Palau has taken a leading regional role in promoting relations with Taiwan, such as hosting the Taiwan-Pacific Allies Summit. During such occasions, Taiwan's sovereignty has been endorsed by the six Pacific governments in attendance, and the subsequent summit declaration has regularly underscored Taiwan's achievements in political democratization and called for Taiwan's participation in international organizations, such as the UN and the World Health Organization.[22]

Palau receives substantial foreign aid, primarily from the United States, Japan, Taiwan, and Australia. For fiscal years 2011 to 2024, U.S. funding support will total $229 million, as well as an estimated $36 million in U.S. federal programs and services. Total U.S. support, including both direct economic assistance and projected discretionary program assistance, may approach a total of $427 million by 2024.[23]

Palau's large infrastructure projects since independence have been varied, and include the road around Babeldaob, the largest island in Palau. U.S. funding for that project was limited to appropriating funds to complete 53 miles of road, with Taiwan agreeing to complete the remainder. One of Japan's most visible aid contributions to Palau is the $25 million Japan Friendship bridge connecting Koror to Babeldaob, which was completed in 2001. Another major endeavor is the Taiwan-funded agricultural-technical mission, intended to advance Palau's domestic agricultural production and reduce food imports. Israel has assisted Palau in a similar manner, with projects focusing on fish farming, as well as in the field of medicine.[24]

Palau has received considerable international attention for an environmental conservation initiative known as the Micronesia Challenge.

---

[22] "Solomon's Sogavare Leads Delegation to Palau Summit," *Solomon Star*, August 31, 2006; and Alexandre Dayant and Jonathan Pryke, "How Taiwan Competes with China in the Pacific," *The Diplomat*, August 9, 2018.

[23] Lum and Vaughn, 2017, p. 10.

[24] U.S. Government Accountability Office (GAO), "Compact of Free Association: Palau's Use of and Accountability for U.S. Assistance and Prospects for Economic Self-Sufficiency," Washington, D.C., June 2008; Wali Osman, *Republic of Palau Economic Report*, Honolulu, Hawaii: East-West Center, 2003; Agnes M. Abrau, "Israel Sending Eye Specialists to Palau," *Palau Horizon*, November 20, 2003.

This involves establishment of a special trust fund intended to conserve 30 percent of a competing nation's marine environment and 20 percent of its terrestrial resources by the year 2020. The FSM, Palau, the RMI, Guam, and the Commonwealth of the Northern Mariana Islands have all agreed to support the challenge with the Netherlands, Germany, Italy, and Spain each making contributions.[25]

Brief History of the Importance of the Freely Associated States to the United States

Since the end of World War II, U.S. knowledge of the history of the FAS and their strategic importance has unfortunately faded.[26] The islands were initially claimed by Spain; Germany was the next claimant, after Spain lost several of its possessions to the United States in the Spanish-American War of 1898. Japan then assumed administrative control over the islands through a League of Nations Mandate. Over the next two decades, Tokyo expanded its control over these small islands through significant settlement and agricultural development. After Japan withdrew from the League of Nations over disputes involving Manchuria, it made the islands "closed territories," restricted access to these islands, and fortified them.

The many islands and atolls provided airfields and deepwater lagoon anchorages that contributed to sea and air control, making them valuable for both power projection eastward, to Midway and Hawaii, and southward to Indonesia and Australia. These fortified islands also offered Tokyo some measure of protection against Allied forces, as

---

25 "Micronesian Challenge: A Shared Commitment to Conserve," webpage, 2012; Cherrie Anne E. Villahermosa, "CNMI Bill Would Fulfill Commitment to Micronesian Challenge," Pacific Islands Development Program, East-West Center, December 3, 2015..

26 This is true for other U.S.-affiliated territories throughout the greater Pacific Ocean area, including Guam, the Commonwealth of the Northern Marianas, and American Samoa, as well as other strategic military sites in World War II, such as Wake and Midway.

demonstrated by the slow and bloody "island hopping" campaign the United States conducted to reverse Japanese expansion in Asia.[27]

After the war, the newly established UN placed what would eventually become the FAS countries and the Commonwealth of the Northern Mariana Islands under the Trust Territory of the Pacific Islands (TTPI).[28] In practice, the U.S. Navy protected the islands, operating from Guam. By 1951, the U.S. Department of the Interior assumed administrative control, and following decades of steady criticism of U.S. management of its trustee responsibilities, the COFA emerged in the 1980s.

Palau signed a 50-year COFA with the United States in 1982, though it did not come into force until 1994, when Palau gained full sovereignty.[29] The COFA with Palau requires a review on the 15-year, 30-year, and 40-year anniversaries of its entering into force. In 2010, the governments of the United States and Palau signed an extension to the agreement as a result of the 15-year review—though the review agreement was only officially authorized in 2017,[30] and entered into

---

[27] For more on the geostrategic importance of FAS from an historical context, see, for example, Walter B. Harris, "The South Sea Islands Under Japanese Mandate," *Foreign Affairs*, July 1932; Pacific War Online Encyclopedia, "Mandates," 2012; Jeter A. Iseley and Philip A. Crowl, *U.S. Marines and Amphibious Warfare*, Princeton, N.J.: Princeton University Press, 1951, pp. 25–26, 76.

[28] The TTPI comprised what are now the Commonwealth of the Northern Mariana Islands, RMI, FSM, and Palau. At the time, the Allies apparently thought that the TTPI arrangement was best because it would avoid fueling the anger of defeated countries, potentially leading to further warfare, as in Germany after World War I.

[29] David Gootnick, *Compacts of Free Association: Issues Associated with Implementation in Palau, Micronesia, and the Marshall Islands*, U.S. Government Accountability Office, Washington, D.C., April 5, 2016, pp. 3–6. The COFA with Palau expires in 2044. However, the 50-year duration should be viewed as a "minimum term." See Ronald Reagan, "Message to the Congress Transmitting Proposed Legislation to Approve the Compact of Free Association with Palau," message to the Congress of the United States, April 9, 1986.

[30] David Gootnick, *Compact of Free Association: Proposed U.S. Assistance to Palau Through Fiscal Year 2024*, U.S. Government Accountability Office, Washington, D.C., September 10, 2012, p. 2; U.S. Department of the Interior, "Secretary Zinke Praises President Trump and Congress for Authorizing Palau Compact Agreement in FY 2018 NDAA," press release, December 13, 2017. In the absence of official authorization, the U.S. provided $79 million in

force in September 2018.[31] Compacts with the FSM and the RMI came into force in 1986. Though their relationship of free association with the United States was and remains indefinite, some COFA provisions were slated to expire in 2001.[32] Between 1999 and 2001, the U.S. negotiated amended COFAs with RMI and FSM that entered into force in 2004 and provided the RMI and the FSM with an additional 20 years of direct financial assistance.[33] Elsewhere in the region, Guam became an unincorporated territory of the United States in 1951. And a separate Covenant between the Commonwealth of the Northern Mariana Islands and the United States came into effect in 1975, making the Commonwealth effectively a U.S. territory.[34] These agreements ended the TTPI.

Terms of the Compacts of Free Association

The Compacts are unique international agreements governing the bilateral relationships between the United States and the FAS. As noted above, the Compacts confer some measure of autonomy to the FAS in exchange for a U.S. defense commitment, significant economic assistance, and other benefits. The Compacts are essentially equal to special treaties created to maintain close and mutually beneficial ties.

The idea of "free association" was first established between New Zealand and two neighboring South Pacific nations, the Cook Islands (1965) and Niue (1974). Self-government in free association provided

---

economic assistance to Palau through annual appropriations from FY2011 through FY2016. See Gootnick, 2016, p. 1.

[31] U.S. Department of State, "United States and Palau Sign Agreement to Amend Compact Review Agreement," September 19, 2018.

[32] Gootnick, 2016.

[33] See, for example, "Bush Signs $3.5 Billion Pacific Compact," *Pacific Islands Report*, December 18, 2003.

[34] U.S. Code, Title 48, Section 1801, Approval of Covenant to Establish a Commonwealth of the Northern Mariana Islands, March 24, 1976. Also see Commonwealth of the Northern Mariana Islands Law Revision Commission, "Covenant," undated.

greater sovereignty and independence for the smaller nations, without hindering visa-free movement for residency, employment, or education.[35] With some modifications, this model has served as the basis for the FAS in the North Pacific. Following their independence, the FSM, the RMI, and Palau joined the UN and other international institutions with full membership rights and responsibilities. At the same time, the Compacts in the North Pacific provided for continued U.S. economic assistance and exclusive U.S. military access. Importantly, in keeping with the principles of sovereignty and self-government, each party retains the right to unilaterally withdraw from the free association agreement.[36]

Under the Compacts, the U.S. Department of the Interior's Office of Insular Affairs (OIA) retains overall management responsibility for U.S. financial assistance in the FAS, while the Department of State handles government-to-government relations.[37] At least 60 U.S. agencies and components provide services to these island nations, including for example the Federal Emergency Management Agency, the United States Postal Service, the National Weather Service, the Federal Aviation Administration, the Environmental Protection Agency, the National Oceanic and Atmospheric Administration, Department of Health and Human Services (including the Centers for Disease Control and Prevention), and others.

Key provisions within the Compacts fall into three categories: government relations, economic relations, and security and defense relations.

Government Relations

Each of the Compacts establish their respective countries as self-governing countries with the capacity to conduct their own foreign affairs,

---

[35] While Cook Islanders and Niueans elected their own parliaments and national leaders, they travel internationally with New Zealand passports. This has complicated their desire to have UN representation.

[36] Allen Stayman, *U.S. Territorial Policy: Trends and Current Challenges*, Honolulu, Hawaii: East-West Center, 2009.

[37] Gootnick, 2016, pp. 3–6.

including the right to enter into treaties and other international agreements with foreign governments, regional organizations, and international organizations, so long as such activities do not violate their security and defense obligations under the Compacts (more on this point below). To that end, the FAS have exchanged diplomatic representatives with other nations and hold membership in regional organizations such as the Pacific Islands Forum (PIF) and the Asian Development Bank as well as international organizations such as the UN, the International Monetary Fund, and the World Bank.[38] The Compacts also provide FAS citizens with certain immigration privileges, such as the right to live, work, and study in the United States indefinitely, as well as the right to enter the United States without a visa.[39]

Trade and Economic Assistance

The Compacts provide for the FAS to receive economic assistance from the United States for the purpose of assisting efforts to promote self-sufficiency and budgetary self-reliance. Economic assistance has primarily taken the form of grants and contributions to Compact Trust Funds, as well as discretionary spending by federal agencies, as seen in Figure 2.1. For the FAS, economic assistance supports a variety of sectors, but prioritizes healthcare and education.[40] Direct grant-based economic assistance to the RMI and the FSM is scheduled to cease at the end of FY 2023 (Palau in FY 2024), whereupon disbursements from Compact Trust Funds were intended to provide a source of U.S. support, the impact of which will be highlighted later in this chapter.[41]

---

[38] Stanley O. Roth, "U.S. and the Freely Associated States," testimony before the House Resources Committee and the House International Relations Committee, October 1, 1998.

[39] See U.S. Department of Homeland Security, "Fact Sheet: Status of Citizens of the Republic of Palau," October 26, 2018, and U.S. Department of Homeland Security, "Fact Sheet: Status of Citizens of the Freely Associated States of the Federated States of Micronesia and the Republic of the Marshall Islands," November 3, 2015.

[40] For example, see Title II, Article I, Section 211 in U.S. Department of State, *Compact of Free Association: Agreement between the United States of America and the Marshall Islands, Amending the Agreement of June 25, 1983*, Majuro, Marshall Islands, April 30, 2003b.

[41] "Ebeye Special Needs" grants represent one notable exception to the COFA expiration date. These grants will provide continued funding for DoD facilities at Kwajalein Atoll out

Figure 2.1
U.S. Assistance to the Freely Associated States

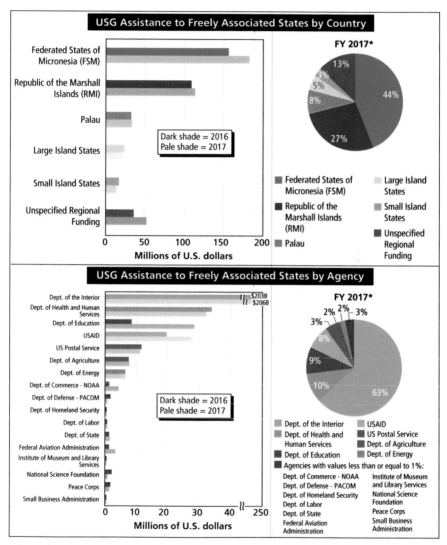

NOTE: The percentages are fairly consistent between FY2016 and FY2017. USG = United States Government; USAID = U.S. Agency for International Development; NOAA = National Oceanic and Atmospheric Administration; PACOM = U.S. Pacific Command.

In fiscal years 1995 through 2009, the U.S. provided $574 million in COFA-related assistance to Palau.[42] A September 2010 agreement between the governments of the United States and Palau extended direct U.S. assistance beyond the initial 15-year period, with $216 million to be allocated annually, in decreasing amounts, from fiscal years 2011 through 2024.[43] Under the terms of the 2010 COFA, the Compact Trust Fund is intended to provide a distribution of $15 million annually to Palau from 2010 to 2044.[44] From fiscal year 2024 onwards, annual grant assistance is scheduled to be terminated—domestic revenue and proceeds from a compact trust fund established under the Compact are slated to take their place in financing Palau's expenditures. As provided for in an amendment to the 2010 agreement, a deposit of approximately $65 million was made to the Compact Trust by the United States in September 2018.[45]

Under the 1986 Compacts with the FSM and the RMI, the United States provided an estimated $2.1 billion in FYs 1987 through 2003.[46] Amended COFAs approved in 2003 resulted in a continuation of direct grant-based financial assistance until fiscal year 2023. Between FY 2003 and FY 2024, the United States expects to provide a total of $3.6 billion in economic assistance to the FSM and the RMI.[47] The grant assistance focuses on education, healthcare, public infrastructure, the environment, public sector capacity building, and the

---

to 2066 or 2086, as long as DoD facilities remain at this location.

[42] All figures are in nominal terms and not adjusted for inflation.

[43] Gootnick, 2012.

[44] Gootnick, 2012, p. 1

[45] U.S. Department of the Interior, "Secretary Zinke Praises U.S. Congress and President Trump for Funding Palau Compact Agreement in the 2018 Omnibus Funding Bill, Provides $123 Million Through 2024," press release, March 26, 2018.

[46] GAO, "Micronesia and the Marshall Islands Continue to Face Challenges Measuring Progress and Ensuring Accountability," Report to the Committee on Energy and Natural Resources, U.S. Senate, September 2013, p. 6.

[47] GAO, "Actions Needed to Prepare for the Transition of Micronesia and the Marshall Islands to Trust Fund Income," Report to the Chairman, Committee on Energy and Natural Resources, U.S. Senate, May 2018.

private sector, prioritizing education and healthcare. The negotiated terms of the amended FSM and RMI Compacts stipulate that annual grant assistance decreases each year leading up to FY 2023, with the difference of the decrease contributed to the Compact Trust Funds, as established under the 2003 amendment.[48] After FY 2023, annual grant assistance will be terminated (except for Palau), and proceeds from the Compact Trust Funds will be utilized for the same six sectors as grants.

The termination of Compact-related grant assistance and the shift to Compact Trust Fund disbursements from FY 2024 onwards is a matter of controversy. Multiple analyses indicate that Compact Trust Fund disbursements will not make up for the budget shortfall expected when grant-based assistance terminates. This is especially the case with the FSM and the RMI. A 2007 study by GAO "found that after fiscal year 2023 the [trust] funds are unlikely to provide maximum annual disbursements, may provide no disbursements at all in some years, and are unlikely to sustain the funds' fiscal year 2023 value."[49] GAO once again reached these conclusions in a follow-up study released in 2018, which found that "the trust funds are increasingly likely to provide no annual disbursements in some years and to not sustain their value."[50] Palau faces a similar predicament. According to the International Monetary Fund (IMF), Palau will need to increase domestic revenue and reduce spending in order to ensure long-term fiscal sustainability after grants expire in 2024.[51] Unless the FAS find alternative sources of financial assistance or take drastic fiscal measures, the expiration of direct grant-based assistance in 2024 will risk undermining their economies.

---

[48] GAO, 2018.

[49] GAO, 2013, p. 23.

[50] GAO, 2018. The GAO study further noted that "Potential strategies such as reduced trust fund disbursements or additional contributions from the countries or other sources could help address these risks. Changing the trust fund disbursement policies could also address these risks but may require revising the trust fund agreements with each country."

[51] International Monetary Fund, "Republic of Palau, Selected Issues," IMF Country Report No. 14/111, May 6, 2014.

Security and Defense Relations

The Compacts allow the United States and the FAS to maintain a robust and mutually beneficial security and defense relationship. The Compacts include provisions for indefinite U.S. authority for defense and security matters, denial of access by potential foreign adversaries to the area, U.S. defense sites and operating rights, and service in the U.S. armed forces for FAS citizens. Taken together, the security and defense provisions of the Compacts form an essential foundation for U.S. national security interests in the region. According to the relevant provisions of each country's COFA, the United States holds full authority and responsibility for security and defense matters in or related to the FAS and may conduct within the FAS any activities and operations necessary to exercise its authority and responsibility.[52] The Compacts entitle the United States to sole and unfettered military access to the lands, waterways, and airspace of the FAS. They provide the United States with the option of establishing and using military areas and facilities in the FAS.[53] However, the United States may not declare war on behalf of the individual FAS, is not allowed to use nuclear, chemical, or biological weapons in their territory, and is not allowed to store such weapons "except in times of national emergency, state of war, or when necessary to defend against an actual or impending attack on the U.S., the Marshall Islands, or the Federated States of Micronesia." These guidelines provide important constraints on U.S. military activities.

One prominent example is the U.S. Army Garrison at the RMI's Kwajalein Atoll (USAKA).[54] Under the Military Use and Operating

---

[52] See Title III, Article I, Section 311 in U.S. Department of State, *Compact of Free Association: Agreement between the United States of America and the Marshall Islands, Amending the Agreement of June 25, 1983*, Majuro, Marshall Islands, April 30, 2003a.

[53] See Title III, Article II in U.S. Department of State, 2003a.

[54] During the Cold War, the RMI was the site of early U.S. nuclear weapons testing. Washington tested nuclear weapons there from 1946 to 1972, prior to the Marshall Islands becoming an independent country in 1986. Operation Crossroads at Bikini Atoll in 1946 included two tests of plutonium weapons, one underwater and the other at a low altitude. The underwater test produced unexpected levels of contamination and unanticipated effects on public health. Crossroads and subsequent tests rendered Bikini Atoll uninhabitable, and

Rights Agreement (MUORA), a subsidiary government-to-government agreement of the amended COFA, the RMI permits continued use of the missile test range until 2066, with an option to extend until 2086.[55] The garrison hosts the Reagan Test Site, the Air Force's Space Fence, the Air Force's Global Positioning System, and Missile Defense Agency tenant organizations, among others. The MUORA permits the garrison to maintain facilities on 11 islands in the atoll and to control entry and movement of personnel into a mid-atoll safety corridor during missile testing. USAKA is the only sustained U.S. military presence in the FAS.

While the Compacts stipulate that the FAS are free to conduct their own foreign affairs, they must refrain from actions deemed by the United States as incompatible with its authority and responsibility for security and defense matters.[56] Significantly, the Compacts forbid the FAS from allowing foreign militaries to enter the islands without U.S. permission.[57] As a consequence of these security and defense provisions, the Compacts deny an enormous and strategically important section of the Western Pacific to potential U.S. adversaries, while enabling U.S. presence and power projection in the region.

Finally, the Compacts establish the eligibility of FAS citizens to serve in the U.S. armed forces. Citizens of the FAS actively participate in U.S. coalition missions and U.S.-led combat operations. According to the U.S. Department of State, FAS citizens serve in the U.S. military at higher per-capita rates than all of the individual states.[58] In return for such generous rights in the FAS, Washington, by law, is responsible for defending from attack the three countries of the FAS and their people. In essence, the Compacts provide the FAS with security assurances similar to an alliance with the United States.

---

had measurable deleterious effects on life expectancy in the Marshall Islands; citizens of the RMI, even today, live with the legacy of these Cold War experiments. Thus, a major subsidiary agreement to the RMI COFA provides for settlement of all claims arising from the U.S. nuclear tests at Bikini and Eniwetok Atolls.

[55] U.S. Department of State, 2003b.

[56] See Title III, Article I, Section 313 in U.S. Department of State, 2003a.

[57] See Title III, Article I, Section 315 in U.S. Department of State, 2003a.

[58] Daniel Russel, "The Freely Associated States," *State Magazine*, April 2016.

CHAPTER THREE

China's Interests and Influence in Oceania and the Freely Associated States

This chapter considers the FAS within the wider context of Beijing's overall approach to the Pacific island states. It also provides a snapshot of some key issues in China's diplomatic and economic activities with each of the FAS.

China's Interests in the Broader Pacific

Pacific island nations have witnessed China's rise, and Beijing has made significant strides in the region as a major trade, aid, investment, and diplomatic partner. While six Pacific island nations continue to recognize Taiwan, Chinese companies are nevertheless increasingly active in these countries, across a broad range of commercial ventures.[1] For example, China is the Solomon Islands' largest trading partner, even though the government of the Solomon Islands has long maintained formal diplomatic links with Taiwan.[2] Tourism from China has increased sharply across Oceania, with Palau and the U.S.-administered Commonwealth of the Northern Marianas being among the most popular destinations in the northwest Pacific. High-profile infrastructure

---

[1] The FSM, Papua New Guinea, Vanuatu, Fiji, Tonga, and Samoa recognize China, while RMI, Palau, Nauru, Tuvalu, the Solomon Islands, and Kiribati recognize Taiwan. The Cook Islands and Niue are represented through New Zealand, and therefore recognize China.

[2] Alexander Simoes, "The Observatory of Economic Complexity," Massachusetts Institute of Technology, 2017.

projects built by Chinese interests, including roads, stadiums, hospitals, and residences for government officials, are found in the countries that maintain official bilateral relations with China. In the subregion of Oceania known as Melanesia, Chinese-owned firms are engaged in resource extraction, such as logging and land-based mining.[3] Chinese commercial ventures have also shown an interest in the emerging field of deep-seabed mining.[4]

China's desire to erode Taiwan's influence in the international space is a key driver of its activities in the Pacific. After Latin America and the Caribbean, Oceania holds the largest grouping of countries recognizing Taiwan, accounting for more than a third of Taiwan's remaining diplomatic allies. These states include Kiribati, Nauru, the Solomon Islands, Tuvalu, Palau, and the RMI. Within the Pacific itself, China appears to view Taiwan's diplomatic allies not only within the context of its longstanding competition with Taiwan, but also as an impediment to Chinese efforts to develop ties and exert influence more generally.

Recent reports about Chinese interest in establishing a military presence in Oceania, combined with Chinese military activities in Southeast Asia, have given rise to concerns among other governments in the region that Beijing's plans may include activities that go beyond robust diplomatic representation and "soft power" public diplomacy. Concerns about potential Chinese efforts to establish a military base in Fiji reportedly contributed to the Australian government agreeing to build a regional hub for police and peacekeeping training there.[5] Canberra has similarly been concerned by media reports on Beijing's

---

[3] Melanesia is one of three subregions of Oceania. The others are Micronesia and Polynesia. Melanesia includes the Solomon Islands, Fiji, Vanuatu, Papua New Guinea, and New Caledonia.

[4] Smith and Porter, eds., *China in Oceania: Reshaping the Pacific?* New York: Berghahn Books, 2010.

[5] Christopher Mudaliar, "Australia Outbids China to Fund Fiji Military Base," *The Interpreter*, October 4, 2018.

interest in establishing a military base on Vanuatu.[6] While the provisions of the Compacts in the North Pacific preclude a Chinese military presence without the concurrence of the United States, neighboring countries in proximity to the FAS do not face similar requirements.

Chinese Economic Assistance Throughout Oceania

China's activities in the Pacific region are driven, in part, by its economic interests. For Beijing, Oceania represents an additional market for Chinese-produced goods.[7] Beijing's economic engagement with the Pacific is spurred by demand for natural resources to fuel its economic growth. According to Xu Xiujun of the Chinese Academy of Social Sciences (CASS), the Pacific holds an abundance of flora, fauna, and mineral resources that could contribute to China's economic development.[8] In addition, most Pacific countries are economically underdeveloped, with unmet needs in education, health, and infrastructure that provide strong incentives for Chinese companies to invest in the region.

Although neither China nor Taiwan participate in the Australian-led "Cairns Compact" initiative for official development assistance (ODA) coordination, evaluation, and transparency in the Pacific, there is little doubt among Pacific island aid specialists that Taiwan's overall aid program in Oceania as a whole pales in comparison to Chinese aid. The Lowy Institute, an Australian think tank, estimates that over the last seven years, China has spent nearly five times as much as Taiwan in the region. The most-comprehensive estimates suggest China has spent $1.26 billion, while Taiwan has expended $224 million.[9] More-

---

[6] David Wroe, "China Eyes Vanuatu Military Base in Plan with Global Ramifications," *Sydney Morning Herald*, April 9, 2018.

[7] Xu Xiujun [徐秀军], "The Diplomatic Strategy of China to Develop the Relations with the South Pacific Region [中国发展南太平洋地区关系的外交战略]," *Pacific Journal* [太平洋学报], Vol. 22, No. 11, November 2014, p. 22.

[8] Xu, 2014, p. 22.

[9] Lowy Institute information cited in Michael Nguyen and Jonathan Pryke, "Exploring Taiwan's Aid to the Pacific," Lowy Institute, September 25, 2018.

over, on average, China's ODA projects are reported to be some nine times larger than Taiwanese projects. Yet, from another perspective, Lowy's analysis has also found that because the countries that recognize Taiwan generally have much smaller populations (with the Solomon Islands being the exception), when viewed on a per capita basis, Taipei spends $237 to Beijing's $108.[10] Among the Pacific countries with smaller populations, such figures may play a role in the calculations of policy makers.

China has shown little serious interest in cooperation with traditional Pacific development partners. For example, an effort by New Zealand's aid agency to include China in a tripartite water project in the Cook Islands has encountered challenges and setbacks.[11] Perhaps the most explicit articulation of China's approach to ODA in the Pacific was made at the 2012 PIF meeting held in the Cook Islands, conveyed by then–Vice Foreign Minister Cui Tiankai of China. Comparing Beijing's position with the broadly embraced Cairns Compact, Cui stated that China's bilateral assistance is qualitatively different. Beijing views its increasing level of engagement as "South-South" aid, or aid from a developing country to another developing country. As such, China likely has no intention of joining with other development partners, and will continue to chart its own independent course with Pacific island nations.[12] The principles of "South-South" cooperation—equality, mutual benefit, common development and non-conditionality—have long been articulated by China as the basis for the ODA globally.

The topic of ODA debt has also become a topic of concern with regard to China. Pacific countries, including Tonga, Vanuatu, and Papua New Guinea, are said to have taken out significant "soft loans" from China for infrastructure. Reuters' analysis of the financial books

---

[10] Lowy Institute, 2018.

[11] Jackie Frizelle, "The Tripartite Cook Islands/China New Zealand Water Project in the Cook Islands—A New Zealand Perspective," New Zealand Ministry of Foreign Affairs & Trade: Aid Programme, undated; and Dateline Pacific, "Cook Islands Drives World-First NZ-China Aid Project," *Radio New Zealand*, October 7, 2013.

[12] Finin, Gerard A., *Power Diplomacy at the 2011 Pacific Islands Forum*, Washington, D.C.: East-West Center, 2011.

of 11 South Pacific island nations shows that over the past decade, China's lending has gone from almost zero to over $1.3 billion.[13] Tonga may be particularly vulnerable, having borrowed heavily in the early 2000s and then having convinced China in 2013 to suspend principal repayments for five years. Although it has asked China for debt forgiveness, Tonga still plans to repay $5.7 million of the $115 million owed to China, a significant portion of its recurrent budget.[14] The Center for Global Development, in a study of lending from China's BRI, found that eight recipient countries outside of the Pacific are at risk of debt distress, including the Indian Ocean island nation of Maldives.[15] The study found that possible leverage associated with such debt, as well as the burdens of debt service payments, has the potential to limit Pacific governments' future expenditures on basic needs.

Courting Taiwan's Remaining Diplomatic Allies

China's desire to erode Taiwan's international space is a key driver of its activity in the Pacific. Multiple Chinese analysts note the concentration of countries recognizing the legitimacy of the Taiwan in the region. According to Xu Xiujun, the Pacific is a "key area for the Taiwan authorities to expand their 'diplomatic space'," given China's past absence from the region.[16]

During the Ma Ying-jeou administration in Taiwan, an unofficial diplomatic truce existed that saw neither China nor Taiwan poach the other's diplomatic allies. Since Tsai Ing-wen of the traditionally independence-leaning Democratic Progressive Party (DPP) won the

---

[13] Charlotte Greenfield and Jonathan Barrett, "Payment Due: Pacific Islands in the Red as Debts to China Mount," *Reuters*, July 30, 2018.

[14] Greenfield and Barrett, 2018. For Tonga's request to China for debt relief, see Stephen Dziedzic, "Tonga Called on Pacific Islands to Band Together Against China—Then Had a Sudden Change of Heart," *Australian Broadcasting Corporation*, August 19, 2018.

[15] See John Hurley, Scott Morris, and Gailyn Portelance, *Examining the Debt Implications of the Belt and Road Initiative from a Policy Perspective*, Washington, D.C.: Center for Global Development, March 2018.

[16] Xu, 2014, p. 19.

2016 election, however, the truce has collapsed. In the last two years alone, Taiwan has lost its diplomatic recognition from, São Tomé and Príncipe (2016), Panama (2017), Burkina Faso (2018), the Dominican Republic (2018), and El Salvador (2018). Within the FAS, both Palau and the RMI recognize Taiwan, and thus are targets of Chinese pressure to switch their recognition. According to Zhang Ying of the Beijing Foreign Studies University, with the rise of the DPP in Taiwan, "China . . . must increase its diplomatic offensive and influence . . . to counter Taiwan independence forces."[17] From Xu Xiujun's point of view, using economics and trade will "enhance [China's] influence and narrow the international living space of 'Taiwan independence' forces."[18] Xing Ruili of Nanjing University's School of International Relations specifically cites the linkage of the BRI with the Pacific as a means of reducing Taiwan's international space.[19]

Chinese president Xi Jinping's visit to Port Moresby, Papua New Guinea, for the Asia Pacific Economic Cooperation (APEC) summit in November 2018 offered a key opportunity for China to emphasize how its potentially transformational projects, such as the BRI, will benefit its diplomatic allies. Xi, for instance, proposed $4 billion in road construction for APEC host Papua New Guinea.[20]

In advancing its "One China" policy, China has gone well beyond dollar diplomacy. China has worked equally hard to cultivate Pacific island leaders through public displays of respect that appear to be designed to expand its diplomatic influence. The extensive protocol and high-level access to Chinese leaders during FAS leaders' official visits to Beijing is widely noted across the region, and consistent with

---

[17] Zhang Ying [张颖], "China's Strategic Choice in the South Pacific: Perspectives, Motivations and Paths [中国在南太平洋地区的战略选择:视角、动因与路径]," *Contemporary World and Socialism*, No. 6, 2016, p. 133.

[18] Xu, 2014, p. 21.

[19] Xing Ruili [邢瑞利], "Progress, Challenges, and Responses of the 'Belt and Road Initiative' in the South Pacific" ["一带一路" 倡议在南太平洋地区的进展、挑战及应对], *Journal of Boundary and Ocean Studies* [边界与海洋研究], No. 3, 2018, p. 95.

[20] John Lee, "China Hoped for a Soft Power Win at APEC, Instead Xi Jinping Left Dissatisfied," *CNN*, November 19, 2018.

the practices often reserved for larger nation states. This level of attention and protocol far exceeds the efforts of the United States and other countries along these lines.

Role of the Pacific in Chinese Defense Strategy

In comparison with other areas of geostrategic importance, such as the South China Sea, publicly available Chinese analysis focusing specifically on the FAS is lacking—reflective of the traditional neglect of this part of the Pacific as a whole in Chinese strategic thinking. According to Chen Xulong, director of the Department of International and Strategic Studies at the China Institute of International Studies (CIIS), the region was largely "inconsequential to Chinese geostrategy and security in the last century."[21]

Nevertheless, Chinese analysts increasingly view the Pacific region as closely tied to China's national security interests. Chen opines that the region's importance has transformed from irrelevance over the last century to "a new historical height, creating considerable prospects for . . . cooperation."[22] The region's strategic location astride major maritime passageways, abundance in certain natural resources, and political power as a voting bloc in international organizations lend it growing value in Chinese foreign policy, particularly as China's overseas interests and influence expand. That statements from the highest levels of the Chinese foreign policy apparatus characterize the Pacific as a natural fit for extending the maritime components of Beijing's BRI suggest the high importance accorded to the region.[23]

---

[21] Chen Xulong [陈须隆], "The Importance and Function of the Pacific Island Countries to China's National Security [太平洋岛国对中国国家安全的重要性及作用]," China Institute of International Studies, February 6, 2015; CIIS is a think tank directly administered by China's Ministry of Foreign Affairs.

[22] Chen, 2015.

[23] See, for example, "Xi Jinping Holds Talks with New Zealand Prime Minister John Key," *Xinhua*, November 20, 2014; and Yang Jiechi [杨洁篪], "Deepen Mutual Trust, Strengthen Docking, and Build a 21st Century Maritime Silk Road [深化互信、加强对接, 共建21世

Along with Northeast Asia, Southeast Asia, South Asia, Central Asia, and West Asia, Chinese analysts perceive the Pacific as one of the so-called "six major sectors" relevant to China's peripheral diplomacy.[24] According to Qi Huaigao and Shi Yuanhua of Fudan University's Institute of International Studies, the Pacific is a strategic extension of Southeastern China.[25] Xu Xiujun, a senior fellow at CASS, concurs, noting that security developments in the region directly affect China's own external security environment.[26] Therefore, Chinese activities in the Pacific are, in part, driven by the need to achieve a stable periphery that is beneficial to China's national interests.

Chinese analysts identify two types of security threats that are prominent in the region. The first entails nontraditional threats such as political instability, piracy, terrorism, transnational crime, and natural disasters, among others. As the world's second-largest economy and largest trading nation, nontraditional security threats could exert an adverse impact on China's economic development. The second type of threat entails the threat of geostrategic encirclement by the United States and its allies.

Some Chinese observers have highlighted what they see as the geostrategic value of the region. As part of the Second Island Chain, some Chinese scholars view the islands of the Pacific as forming a natural barrier to China's maritime expansion into the open ocean. Fudan University scholar Qi Huaigao outlines how one school of contemporary Chinese foreign policy thinking views the development of ties in the Pacific as necessary to achieve "maritime breakthroughs" past encircling external powers.[27] Zhang Ying, of the Beijing Foreign Stud-

---

纪海上丝绸之路]," speech delivered at the Boao Forum for Asia, Bo'ao, China, March 29, 2015.

[24] For an early outline of the "six major sectors," see Qi Huaigao [祁怀高] and Shi Yuanhua [石源化], "China's Peripheral Security and Greater Peripheral Diplomatic Strategy [中国周边安全与大周边外交战略]," *CNKI Journal*, No. 6, 2013.

[25] Qi and Shi, 2013, p. 44.

[26] Xu, 2014, p. 21.

[27] Qi Huaigao [祁怀高], "Thoughts on the Top Design of Periphery Diplomacy [关于周边外交顶层设计的思考]," *Journal of International Relations* [国际关系研究], Forum of

ies University, writes that the "South Pacific region [likely not including the FAS, but still instructive of Chinese regional views] . . . hinders China's expansion into the deep sea," an opinion shared by Xu Xiujun.[28] Xu adds that U.S. military presence in the region will very likely play a key role in U.S. efforts to contain China.

While recognizing the region's potential as a bulwark against China's rise, some Chinese analysts are adamantly against matching demonstrations of hard power by the United States in the Pacific. Qi Huaigao and Shi Yuanhua argue for a "diplomatic" approach that would "reduce U.S., Japanese, European, and [other] interference in [its] South Pacific policy."[29] Echoing Norwegian China watcher Marc Lanteigne, Yu Changshen, of Sun Yat-sen University's National Centre for Oceania Studies, characterizes the U.S.–China regional competition as one of soft balancing, with China likely to focus on cooperative initiatives as opposed to matching U.S. hard power in the region.[30] Xu Xiujun of CASS believes that "national security cannot solely be guaranteed by military power," and China's participation in various regional cooperation mechanisms such as the PIF could "weaken U.S. efforts to strategically surround China in the South Pacific."[31] Ma Feng of the People's Liberation Army's (PLA's) National Defense University takes a similar position, while adding that increased engagement in the South Pacific could relieve strategic pressure in the South China Sea.[32]

World Economics and Politics [世界经济与政治], No. 4, 2014, p. 15.

[28] Zhang, 2016, p. 132; Xu, 2014, p. 21; for an overview of Chinese strategic thinking on island chains, see Andrew S. Erickson and Joel Wuthnow, "Barriers, Springboards and Benchmarks: China Conceptualizes the Pacific 'Island Chains,'" *China Quarterly*, No. 225, March 2016.

[29] Qi and Shi, 2013, p. 45.

[30] Yu Chang Sen, "The Pacific Islands in Chinese Geo-strategic Thinking," paper presented to the conference on China and the Pacific: The View from Oceania, National University of Samoa, February 25–27, 2015; also see Marc Lanteigne, "Water Dragon? China, Power Shifts and Soft Balancing in the South Pacific," *Political Science*, Vol. 64, No. 1, 2012.

[31] Xu, 2014, p. 21.

[32] Ma Feng, "Ma Feng: The South Pacific and the 21st Century Maritime Silk Road [马锋: 南太平洋与21世纪海上丝绸之路]," *Chinese Social Sciences Net*, May 23. 2017.

At least one Chinese observer alludes to the possibility of a long-term military presence in the region. Liang Jiarui, of the Pacific Islands Research Center at Liaocheng University, argues for the establishment of so-called "strategic fulcrum ports" in the Pacific to secure maritime access in the region.[33] These ports can provide the PLA Navy (PLAN) with supply points that would be conducive to reducing the gap in hard power between China and the U.S. in the region.[34] Beijing has also focused on gaining traction through expanding its influence, primarily through diplomatic and economic engagement.

China's Relationship with the Federated States of Micronesia

The FSM established formal diplomatic relations with China in 1989. Since that time, the relationship has grown, including the 2014 creation of the commission on economic trade cooperation.[35] China's economic relationship with the FSM includes substantial trade and aid components. Prior to APEC in 2018, the FSM signed a BRI memorandum of understanding with China, making it the last Pacific country with diplomatic relations to do so. To be sure, the United States and its allies and partners account for considerably more of the FSM's trade than China does. According to the U.S.-China Economic and Security Review Commission report on China's engagement in the Pacific Islands, the FSM's number one trade partner in 2017 was South Korea, with total trade amounting to about $52 million. The United States was second, with about $46 million in total trade. China was third, with about $38 million, followed by Japan at $34 million and Taiwan

33 Liang Jiarui [梁甲瑞], "The Establishment of Strategic Fulcrum Ports and the Security of Strategic Passageways in the South Pacific Region [南太平洋地区海上战略通道安全与战略支点港口的构建]," *Journal of Strategy and Decision-making* [战略决策研究], No. 2, 2017.

34 Liang, 2017, p. 67.

35 Bill Jaynes, "Visit to China by Vice President Yosiwo P. George." *Kaselehlie Press*, October 18, 2018.

at $31 million.[36] This might change, however, with the FSM signing up to the BRI.

Beijing has also accorded a state visit to FSM President Peter Christian—an honor that has had lasting positive effect on the FSM's perception of China. The well-planned trip included a welcome ceremony at the Great Hall of the People in Beijing with a full military review. A photograph showing both presidents being warmly greeted by flag-waving school children as they walked down a red carpet was widely broadcast on social media.[37] Chinese president Xi personally invested a significant amount of time in one-on-one discussions related to economic development.[38] On the subject of tourism, for instance, it was noted that China has endorsed the FSM as an officially sanctioned tourist destination, and was willing to support a range of infrastructure projects related to growing the FSM's fledgling tourism industry. The visit included the announcement of block grants for the four states of the FSM, as well as the gifting of a new inter-island aircraft, which provided media headlines that bolstered China's standing within the FSM.[39]

The appearance of respect and dignity conveyed through such high-profile visits underscores China's strategic interests in the region. There is a clear understanding by political leadership in the Pacific Islands of Beijing's desire to have strong bilateral relationships in the region that will increase its influence. At the same time, official visits—like that of FSM's president to China—provide a basis for comparison with Washington's lack of high-level attention to the FAS and the Pacific region more generally. Underscoring the point, President

---

[36] Meick et al., 2018.

[37] Embassy of the Federated States of Micronesia, Public Information Office, "Official Visit to China by President Peter M. Christian," April 4, 2017.

[38] A more recent example is Samoan Prime Minister Tuilaepa Sailele Malielegaoi's September 2018 participation in the Davos Forum in Northern China. While in Beijing, he held talks with President Xi Jinping, who promised to work with Samoa on climate change issues and deepen ties between the two countries. See, for example, "China Says It Will Help Samoa with Climate Change," *Radio New Zealand*, September 20, 2018.

[39] See Embassy of the Federated States of Micronesia, 2017.

Christian said: "Yeah, China was impressive. If that's the way they welcome other countries[,] [w]e were flattered. I was flattered that for a small country they would exhibit such formality."[40] President Donald Trump's historic decision to host all three FAS leaders at the White House on May 21, 2019, however, demonstrates refocused U.S. attention on this critically important region.

According to interviews, China has a three-pronged approach: diplomatic, military, and private sector (investments). Beijing actively engages with the FSM through investments (especially fisheries). Over the last three decades, China has undertaken a range of projects in the FSM. Chinese embassy–issued discretionary grants frequently provide much-needed civilian equipment to perform a range of tasks. The embassy also occasionally funds larger infrastructure projects, and in many cases, those projects are implemented by Chinese companies with Chinese labor. These have ranged from building official residences for government officials at the national and state levels, to constructing ships for inter-island transport. Block grants for purposes specified by state governments have also been an element of Chinese engagement. Educational institutions have benefited from high-profile projects, such as the popular "FSM–China Friendship Sports Center" gymnasium built at the College of Micronesia in Pohnpei, initially structured as a $3.8 million interest-free loan that was subsequently announced as a grant.[41] Other such small grants and gifts as solar street lights for state capitals and library book donations covering a wide range of subjects on China are frequently noted in media accounts.[42] Direct aid to local FSM governments is valued, because with it comes perceived status and prestige for local officials, some of whom over time will be elected to national offices. In 2016, for instance, the Chinese embassy donated $277,844 for the construction of a new gymnasium complex

---

[40] Bill Jaynes, "FSM President Talks About His State Visit to China," *Kaselehlie Press*, April 20, 2017.

[41] Jaynes, 2017.

[42] See, for example, "China Donates Solar Lights to Pohnpei Municipalities," *Kaselehlie Press*, October 23, 2017.

in Madolenihmw.[43] Meanwhile, a new sign touts the "Kolonia-China Friendship Center" in Kolonia. In Pohnpei State, China has launched a pilot farm in Pohnlangas, as well as greenhouse construction, biogas projects, and a mushroom demonstration farm.[44]

Chinese investors have recently been pushing for a 200-room casino in Pohnpei. The governor backs the plan, and the legislature is now considering it. The most ambitious Chinese investment proposal in the FSM, to date, has been the plan to build a 10,000-room holiday resort and casino complex in the state of Yap, and establish direct airline connections to facilitate ease of travel for vacationers.[45] Announcement of the endeavor in 2011 surprised Yap's citizenry, and gave rise to considerable debate regarding the wisdom of building such a massive resort in a location with a population of 11,000, residing on a relatively small island.[46] The linkages between FSM and China appear to have expanded in 2015, when Yap's governor and a 12-member delegation made an Embassy-arranged ten-day trip to China. A subsequent visit to Yap was made the same year by representatives from the Guangdong Friendship Association and Zhongshan City.[47]

With the neighboring Republic of Palau having attracted nearly 90,000 Chinese tourists in 2016, Yap's potential for increased tourism presented an attractive business opportunity. However, even after the

---

[43] "China Donates Over a Quarter of a Million Dollars for New Madolenihmw Gym," *Kaselehlie Press*, November 4, 2016.

[44] "Pohnpei Governor Gives State of the State Address," *Kaselehlie Press*, March 14, 2018.

[45] University of Guam Professor Donald Rubinstein at a public seminar on May 8, 2014. He indicated that Chengdu Century City New International Exhibition and Convention Center Company Ltd., better known as ETG, proposed the Paradise concept plan. The plan consists of construction of an oceanfront resort complex including artificial offshore islands and bungalows built over the lagoon, golf courses, expanded airport and seaport facilities, "an immense water reservoir system" and native towns where displaced Yapese will be relocated. See Lexi Villegas Zotomayor, "Mega-Casino Resort Project Reportedly 'Still on the Table' in Yap," *Pacific Islands Report*, June 5, 2014.

[46] "Chinese Investors Plan Major Hotel In Yap," *Pacific Islands Report*, October 5, 2011; and "Large-Scale Yap Tourism Development Halted in FSM," *Pacific Islands Report*, September 6, 2012.

[47] See, for example, Concerned Yap Citizens, "Timeline: Governor Ganngiyan and His Delegation Return Home Safely From Week-Long China Visit," website, November 13, 2015.

initial building plans were scaled back, the image of hordes of tourists adversely changing Yap's highly valued traditional culture, as well as the potential environmental impacts, resulted in the temporary shelving of the project. Nonetheless, despite the shelving, a Chinese group called Chengdu Exhibition and Travel Group has leased approximately 25 percent of Yap land, using 99-year leases, renewable automatically for a second term. Some of this land could impede U.S. security and defense responsibilities.[48] To the extent that most FSM citizens do not distinguish between official Chinese government assistance and private-sector initiatives, the controversial proposal seemingly undermined diplomatic efforts by China to show itself as a responsible and culturally sensitive development partner. In 2014, another lower-profile point of friction between Yap and a Chinese firm arose, centered on the illegal harvesting of sea cucumbers *(beche de mer)*. It was also found that the Chinese company had failed to renew its business license during the previous year.[49]

The FSM's engagement with China is also reflected in enhanced diplomatic activities. In August 2017, for example, Chinese Vice Minister of Foreign Affairs Zheng Zeguang visited Pohnpei with a high-level delegation, and spoke to FSM political leaders. A key topic of the dialogue centered on the FSM Trust Fund that the government of the FSM will rely on, in addition to the Compact Trust Fund, after the expiration of U.S. COFA economic assistance in 2023. It was suggested that China might be willing to supplement the Trust Fund to help the FSM achieve greater self-reliance.[50]

Chuuk State, the FSM's largest state (pop. 48,500), has expressed interest in becoming a sovereign nation, recently postponing an independence referendum from 2019 to 2020. This could emerge as an important consideration in the context of China's relationship with the

---

[48] Joyce McClure, "Yap Is Having Serious Second Thoughts About Chinese Tourism [Updated]," Pacific Island Times, January 26, 2018.

[49] "Chinese Firm Has Licenses Revoked for Illegal Sea Cucumber Harvesting," *Pacific Islands Report*, July 14, 2014.

[50] "FSM Receives Visit from Highest Ranked Chinese Official in FSM's History," *Kaselehlie Press*, September 18, 2017.

FSM. Throughout the FSM's history there has been domestic internal contention between the state and the national government over the equitable distribution of non-COFA funding (fisheries and tax revenue). The United States has consistently maintained that its relationship is with the national government in Palikir, and any movement by a state to secede would, if a state were no longer part of the federation, presumably mean an end to the COFA in all its dimensions. While this understanding has implicitly buttressed national unity, the cessation of economic support after FY 2023 may undermine national cohesion. Such a development could have important strategic implications. The Chuuk lagoon, one of the Pacific's largest and deepest, was once a critically important location for the Japanese Navy, and remains a potentially important strategic naval asset.

The vibrant diplomatic linkages between the FSM and China include several "people-to-people" programs. Mechanisms such as "sister city" agreements are being established to strengthen relationships and promote investment. For example, the municipal government of Sokehs in FSM and Zhongshan City of China, although not comparable in size, recently signed a document designed to foster better relations and understanding between citizens of both countries. A similar relationship has been announced with China's Heilongjiang Province for the purposes of advancing supporting promotion, facilitated by a visiting delegation from Heilongjiang province.[51]

China has also provided a steady stream of opportunities for young people. For many years, FSM students have taken advantage of scholarship opportunities in China. In 2017, Hainan Province in China and Yap State established a new sister province-to-state relationship, at which time Hainan made a commitment to provide 50 scholarships within five years for FSM students. In addition, Hainan extended a range of invitations for youth and technical transfer exchanges.[52] Small grants have been provided on a regular basis for athletic activities,

---

[51] Embassy of the Federated States of Micronesia, 2017.

[52] Embassy of the Federated States of Micronesia, 2017.

including travel stipends and transit accommodations to fund the FSM team's participation in the 2016 Olympics in Rio de Janeiro, Brazil.[53]

None of these activities or projects linking China and the FSM are outside the bounds of normal diplomatic and economic engagement, and indeed, the United States and China share a similar range of activities to bolster bilateral relations. But Beijing's intent is clear: to undermine U.S. influence with the FSM. Therefore, a significant diminution of U.S. economic support may erode the strong bonds between the United States and the FSM, thereby undermining the special relationship built over the past seven decades. Several interviewees stated that China seeks to increase its own influence when it perceives U.S. involvement is declining. As such, they predicted that if U.S. support declines, China will likely seek to expand cooperation.

China's Relationship with the Republic of the Marshall Islands

Although it does not receive diplomatic recognition from the RMI, Beijing nevertheless is attempting to increase its influence there, with the ultimate goal of persuading the RMI to shift diplomatic recognition from Taipei to Beijing. Trade is an important part of China's relationship with the RMI, even though the RMI still maintains official diplomatic relations with Taiwan. According to the USCC report on China's engagement in the Pacific Islands, the RMI's top trade partner in 2017 was South Korea, with total trade amounting to about $6.9 billion. China was second, with about $3.1 billion. Japan was third with about $1.3 billion, followed by the United States at $610 million and Taiwan at $131 million.[54]

While the RMI's relationship with the United States helps support the RMI's position vis-à-vis Taipei, China is actively engaged

---

[53] Jim Tobin, "Team FSM to Compete in 2016 Olympic Games in Rio de Janeiro," *Kaselehlie Press*, August 6, 2016.

[54] Meick et al., 2018.

in the local economy, and the fishing industry in particular.[55] China has commercial ties to the RMI through fishing companies such as Pan Pacific Foods. In the absence of official diplomatic recognition of China, the head of Pan Pacific Foods is considered an unofficial Chinese representative to the RMI, according to interviewees.[56] Beijing is also a part owner in the Marshall Islands Fishing Company, another major fishing enterprise in the RMI.

At the Asia World Expo held in Hong Kong in April 2018, a Chinese businessman and the mayor of Rongelap Atoll proposed the creation of a special administrative region to attract investment to the atoll, which is located near the U.S. Ronald Reagan Missile Defense Testing Site at Kwajalein Atoll. The mayor of Rongelap supported turning it into a "special administrative region" and financial center on par with Hong Kong, Singapore, and Dubai.[57] It is unclear the extent to which Beijing might support the proposal, though some observers have suggested that China might be eyeing the location for strategic reasons because of its proximity to Kwajalein.[58] The proposal quickly became a source of controversy in RMI politics, stemming from concerns that such a proposal could make the area a haven for money laundering and other illegal activities; the government declined to back it after it was declared unconstitutional by the RMI Attorney General. In November 2018, President Hilda Heine narrowly survived a no-confidence vote that was ostensibly brought because of opposition to plans to introduce a state-backed cryptocurrency, but President Heine stated that the real reason for the vote was her government's opposition to the Chinese-backed Rongelap plan. "Really the vote of no-confidence is about the so-called Rongelap Atoll Special Administrative Region, or RASAR scheme, which is an effort by certain foreign interests to take control of

---

[55] Louis Harkell, "Marshall Islands Subsidiary of Chinese Firm Orders Three New Tuna Seiners for $62m," *Undercurrentnews*, July 17, 2018; and Mackenzie Smith, "Remote Marshall Islands Atoll Plans to Become the 'Next Hong Kong,'" *Radio New Zealand*, September 21, 2018.

[56] Interview conducted with senior official in Washington, D.C. on October 24, 2018.

[57] Smith, 2018.

[58] Interviews conducted in September–October 2018.

one of our atolls and turn it into a country within your own country," she told Radio New Zealand.[59]

Another issue in China's relationship with the RMI is the RMI's status as the world's third-largest ship registry. Panama remains number one, but the RMI surpassed Liberia for the number two spot in 2017 before recently falling down to third place. Ships entering Chinese ports that are registered in countries that do not recognize China face higher port fees, so the RMI's ship-registry program faces a loss of revenue because China charges higher fees to ships entering its ports flying the RMI flag.[60] Notably, after Panama switched recognition from Taiwan to China, China signed an agreement to offer reduced port fees for ships registered in Panama.[61] Liberia, which previously recognized Taiwan but now recognizes China, also enjoys preferential rates when Liberian-registered ships visit Chinese ports.[62] Consequently, this is a potentially vulnerable pressure point for the RMI, according to interviews.[63]

China has also received a license to conduct seabed mining in an area just outside of the exclusive economic zone (EEZ) of the RMI, which interviewees identified as another potential source of controversy.[64] In addition, Beijing is reportedly offering the prospects of financial assistance via the BRI as a way to convince the RMI to switch official diplomatic relations to China, and there are reports that Beijing is

---

[59] Dateline Pacific, "Marshalls President, Facing Ouster, Blames Chinese Influence," *Radio New Zealand*, November 9, 2018; and Alan Boyd, "Chinese Money Unsettles Marshallese Politics," *Asia Times*, November 14, 2018.

[60] Interviews conducted in September–October 2018.

[61] Wendy Laursen, "Fair Game: The Competition for New Business Heats Up," *Maritime Executive*, September 24, 2017.

[62] Vincent Wee, "China Renews Port Dues Discounts for Liberia Flag Vessels," *Seatrade Maritime News*, September 10, 2018.

[63] Interviews conducted in September–October 2018.

[64] Interview conducted in October 2018.

offering bribes to local politicians with the goal of persuading them to recognize China instead of Taiwan.[65]

China's Relationship with Palau

Trade is an important component of China's relationship with Palau, even though Palau maintains official diplomatic relations with Taiwan rather than China. Nonetheless, the United States and U.S. allies and partners account for a much larger share of Palau's trade. According to the USCC report on China's engagement in the Pacific islands, Palau's top trade partner in 2017 was Japan, with about $50 million in total trade. Taiwan was second at $22 million. The United States was third with about $20 million in trade, followed by China with about $18 million and South Korea with $10 million.[66]

Tourism has been another important component of China's relationship with Palau, which has emerged as a popular destination for visitors from a number of countries. Indeed, it is the vibrancy of Palau's private sector that sets it apart from its neighbors that are also in free association with Washington; much of this is associated with its tourism industry. Drawing on historical linkages and investments from Japan, Palau's tourism industry constructed its first luxury resort in 1985. After independence, efforts were made to diversify its market to attract not only Japanese tourists, but also Koreans and Taiwanese. Palau's diplomatic relations (formalized in 1999) and geographic proximity to Taiwan steadily increased the visitor flows from Taipei, which by 2012 had reached 39,695.[67] However, it was not long before Taiwanese travel agencies realized the potential for working with mainland travel agencies to send even larger numbers of tourists from mainland China.

---

[65] Grant Newsham, "Beijing's Great Game to Win Over Pacific's Small Island States," *Asia Times*, September 7, 2018.

[66] Meick et al., 2018.

[67] Hezel, 2017.

Although the Chinese government never officially allowed Chinese tourist groups to visit Palau, known as an "approved destination status" (ADS) designation, it allowed Chinese tour agents to promote group package tours there via commercial and charter flights. These tour groups rapidly came to constitute the largest share of Palau's tourism industry. Between 2011 and 2015, the number of Chinese tourists soared from 1,699 to 86,850, or more than fifty percent of annual visitor arrivals.[68] In November 2017, the Chinese government ordered tour operators to stop selling package tours to Palau, with a warning that sending tourists to locations without ADS status could lead to substantial fines.[69]

This decline in tourist numbers has already had implications for Palau's economy. Based on 2013 figures, the $41.4 million collected from gross revenue business taxes, personal income taxes, general import taxes, and airport departure green (environmental) fees were nearly equal to the total grant money ($42 million) received from the United States, Taiwan, and multiple other sources.[70] Not unexpectedly, interviews indicate that the key to restoring outbound plane loads of tour groups from China hinges on Palau switching diplomatic relations from Taiwan to China.[71] Although Taiwan has increased its support for Palau's tourism industry, its ability to offset the loss of such a large number of Chinese visitors is limited. Palau also hopes tourism from Japan and the United States could help offset the loss of revenue from the decline in the number of Chinese tourists. Interviews and media reports suggest that China's goal is to create a situation in which Palau may conclude that it would be better off shifting official diplomatic recognition from Taipei to Beijing, but Palau has stated that it will maintain its ties with Taiwan.[72]

---

[68] Hezel, 2017.

[69] Kate Lyons, "'Palau Against China!': the Tiny Island Standing Up to a Giant," *Guardian*, September 7, 2018.

[70] Hezel, 2017, p. 39.

[71] Interviews, September–October 2018.

[72] Interviews, September–November 2018. See also "Palau Asks US and Japan for Help After China Imposes 'Tourist Ban' Over Tiny Island's Ties with Taiwan," *South China*

Conclusion

China appears to be attempting to increase its influence in the FAS, likely at the expense of the United States, and it has a number of economic and diplomatic instruments at its disposal. Uncertainty surrounding the future of the COFA assistance grants after FY2023— and FY2024, in the case of Palau—offers Beijing a unique opportunity to continue undermining the FAS' commitment to Washington (as well as to Taiwan for the RMI and Palau) over the next four years. Although none of the FAS are currently considering downgrading ties with the United States, this will depend on the extent to which their vulnerability to Chinese leverage and receptivity to Chinese inducements increases, absent a sustainable way forward on the Compacts' extension.

Morning Post, July 26, 2018; Lauren Beldi, "China's 'Tourist Ban' Leaves Palau Struggling to Fill Hotels and an Airline in Limbo," *ABC News*, August 27, 2018; and "Palau Tourism Industry 'Suffering Greatly' from China Ban," *Radio New Zealand*, September 3, 2018.

CHAPTER FOUR

Activities and Responses of Other Countries in Oceania and the Freely Associated States

A number of other countries have interests in Oceania and the FAS, and China's rising profile in the region as a whole has prompted other regional states with traditional interests in the Pacific to react. This chapter examines the responses and activities undertaken by Australia, New Zealand, Taiwan, and Japan, which complement U.S. objectives and present opportunities for multilateral engagement and assistance with the FAS.

Australia

Australia has played a relatively limited role in the FAS, but it has been very active in the broader region. Indeed, Australia has traditionally been the dominant player in Oceania as well as the region's primary trading partner and aid donor. It is also a founding member of key regional organizations like the PIF, the Secretariat of the Pacific Community (formerly called the South Pacific Commission), the Forum Fisheries Agency, and the Secretariat of the Pacific Regional Environment Program. And besides its historical ties with the United Kingdom, Australia's relationship with the Pacific is the only relationship specifically mentioned in its constitution. Due to a combination of geography and linkages in trade and investment, tourism, aid, and sports, Australia has maintained this relationship with its regional neighbors for decades. Its engagement, however, has been characterized by periods of apathy, interspersed with spikes of intense engagement.[1]

Australia's Activities and Interests in the Broader Oceania Region

Canberra's interest is largely driven by security concerns. Given the region's geographic proximity to Australia and position along Australia's maritime trade routes, Canberra's primary concerns are instability or underdevelopment potentially affecting Australia's security should refugees, humanitarian disasters, or manmade crises spill over into the region. And in its 2013 National Security Strategy, Canberra highlighted a newer concern, which was the risk of "another state seeking to influence Australia or its regional and global partners by economic, political or military pressure."[2] In light of this view, Australia has an interest in helping the Pacific Islands to maintain regional stability and ensure "no other major power whose interests may be different to Australia's puts undue or coercive pressure on small countries where Australian influence is traditionally dominant."[3]

Because of Australia's interests, Australia is the largest donor in the broader Pacific region. From 2006 to 2013, it provided $6.83 billion in aid to the region, more than the next four donors combined,[4] and remains the largest aid provider to the Pacific Islands. Using data from the Lowy Institute's project on Pacific aid, in the last year of complete data collected (2016), Australia's annual aid to the region stood at $798.7 million.[5] The government's investments focus on better water supply, improvements in early grade learning, gender equality and more-reliable internet services.

---

[1] Greg Colton, "Safeguarding Australia's Security Interests Through Close Pacific Ties," Lowy Institute, April 2018.

[2] Department of the Prime Minister and Cabinet, Government of Australia, *Strong and Secure: A Strategy for Australia's National Security*, Canberra, Australia, 2013.

[3] Jenny Hayward-Jones, "The Pacific Islands Play the Field," *The Diplomat*, No. 26, January 2017, p. 2

[4] Philippa Brant, "Chinese Aid in the Pacific," Lowy Institute for International Policy, February 2015.

[5] Lowy Institute, "Pacific Aid Map," webpage, 2018.

Prime Minister Malcolm Turnbull announced in 2016 that Australia would "step up" engagement in the Pacific.[6] This was followed up in 2017 by the Minister for Foreign Affairs, Julie Bishop, announcing three goals to strengthen Australia's engagement: stronger partnerships for economic growth, stronger partnerships for security, and supportive relationships between the people of Australia and the region.[7] These were laid out in Australia's 2016 Defense White Paper and 2017 Foreign Policy White Paper, which both place significant importance on the Pacific Islands. The 2016 Defense White Paper states that Australia's strategic defense interests include a "secure nearer region."[8] The White Paper goes on to focus on the Pacific Islands specifically: "The Government will work with Pacific Island Countries to strengthen their ability to manage internal, transnational and border security challenges . . . [including] working to limit the influence of any actor from outside the region with interests inimical to our own."[9] Similarly, the Foreign Policy White Paper states that security in these states "is vital to our ability to defend Australia's northern approaches, secure our borders and protect our exclusive economic zone."[10] More recently, Australia and the United States announced plans to redevelop a naval base on Papua New Guinea's Manus Island, a move widely viewed as aimed at balancing China's growing influence in the region.[11]

Australia's Activities and Influence in the Freely Associated States
Australia's role in the FAS is limited, however. Australia's diplomatic footprint in the FAS is much smaller than elsewhere in the broader

---

6   Malcolm Turnbull, "Helping Our Neighbours," September 8, 2016.

7   Julie Bishop, "Australia in the Pacific," speech delivered in Fiji, August 12, 2017.

8   Australian Government, Department of Defence, *2016 Defence White Paper*, Canberra: Commonwealth of Australia, 2016.

9   Australian Government, Department of Defence, 2016.

10   Australian Government, *2017 Foreign Policy White Paper*, Canberra: Department of Foreign Affairs and Trade, 2017.

11   Natalie Whiting, "Joint Australian-U.S. Naval Base on Manus Island a 'Significant Pushback' against China's Pacific Ambitions," *Australian Broadcasting Corporation*, November 18, 2018.

region. Its sole regional ambassador, located in the FSM, has multiple accreditations: to the FSM, the RMI, and Palau, and (as Consul-General) to Guam and the Commonwealth of the Northern Mariana Islands. Australia is, however, planning to open diplomatic posts in both Palau and the RMI by 2020.[12] Notably, in the security domain, Canberra in June 2014 unveiled its $1.88 billion Pacific Patrol Boat Program, which included all of the FAS, giving it additional leverage in the regional security domain.[13]

Australia's ODA is also much less than in other parts of the Pacific. Australia's ODA to the Compact states represents a very small share of Australia's total ODA, but is nonetheless significant.[14] The most recent data show that in the 2018–2019 timeframe, Australia will provide Palau, the FSM, and the RMI with an estimated $8 million in aid.[15] While the aid itself focuses on women's social and economic empowerment in all three countries, as part of Canberra's Pacific Women Shaping Pacific Development program, it also is directed toward specific purposes in each state.[16] For FSM, it is directed at improving the quality of basic education. In RMI, it is intended for clean water and sanitation, and in Palau, for reliable internet services. While Australia's aid to the Pacific region as a whole is the largest, in 2016 it was only the third largest donor to Palau ($1.89 million) and the fourth largest donor to RMI ($4.05 million).[17]

[12] Scott Morrison, "Australia and the Pacific: A New Chapter," address delivered to troops in Lavarack Barracks in Townsville, Queensland, Australia, November 8, 2018.

[13] Shahryar Pasandideh, "Australia Launches New Patrol Boat Program," *The Diplomat*, July 1, 2014.

[14] Australian Government, Department of Foreign Affairs and Trade, "North Pacific Aid Fact Sheet," October 2018.

[15] Australian Government, 2018. This is a large amount, but still represents a reduction. In the 2016–2017 timeframe, Australian ODA to the North Pacific was $10.7 million.

[16] Pacific Women, "Pacific Women: Shaping Pacific Development," webpage, 2017; Australian Government, 2018.

[17] Lowy Institute, 2018.

New Zealand

Like Australia, New Zealand is a resident power with vested interests in the Pacific Islands. And like Australia, while New Zealand tends to focus on the Pacific Islands as a grouping, rather than individual states, its focus has not been the COFA states. Instead, it has focused on the South Pacific or regional organizations. However, Wellington is a leading donor to the broader region. From 2006 to 2013, it was the fourth-largest donor, providing nearly $1.1 billion.[18] And in 2016, the most recent year with complete data, Wellington was the second-largest donor to all Pacific island nations—behind Canberra—at over $192 million (these numbers, however, appear to discount U.S. economic assistance under the Compacts, which is at least $350 million a year).[19]

New Zealand's Activities and Interests in the Broader Oceania Region

Wellington's involvement with the FAS needs to be viewed in the larger context of its Pacific Island engagement. Wellington's officially stated interest in the Pacific is a desire to "improve the prosperity, stability and resiliency of the region and its people."[20] Further, New Zealand's "strong cultural and historical ties" with these countries, "and the potential for any adverse security situation to impact on New Zealand or New Zealanders, underpin its enduring interest in the region."[21] This is mirrored by similar language used by the Ministry of Foreign Affairs and Trade, which details "three primary prisms" through which New Zealand views its Pacific engagement: identity, security, and prosperity.[22]

---

[18] Brant, 2015.

[19] Lowy Institute, 2018.

[20] Brook Barrington, "MFAT Annual Review 2016/17," remarks made to the Foreign Affairs, Defence and Trade Select Committee, Canberra, Australia, February 28, 2018.

[21] "North Pacific Development Fund," New Zealand Foreign Affairs and Trade, webpage, undated.

[22] "Pacific," New Zealand Foreign Affairs & Trade, webpage, undated.

Similar to Australia, New Zealand has a great interest in regional stability. As competition grows for scarce fisheries and other marine resources, there are more foreign vessels operating in the EEZs of New Zealand and its neighbors. Additionally, given its proximity to Antarctica and concerns over the existential threat posed by rising sea levels, the adverse effects of climate change are high among Wellington's concerns, as these effects could lead to instability within Pacific Islands countries and territories, and spill over to affect New Zealand. New Zealand differs from Australia and Japan, however, because it lacks the large economic resources that those countries use in their foreign engagement. And, in recent years, under-investment in the Pacific has left Wellington open to criticism that it had abandoned its neighborhood.

Reacting to those criticisms of abandonment amidst rising concerns that the Pacific is becoming an increasingly contested strategic space, Wellington announced a "Pacific Reset" in March 2018.[23] Centered around five core principles—friendship, understanding, mutual benefit, collective ambition. and sustainability—the Reset is meant to increase New Zealand's engagement to the Pacific region.[24] This is to be done through renewed diplomacy and increased aid. Thus far, the most visible pillar of the Reset has been its aid program. About 60 percent of New Zealand's total aid goes to the Pacific region, accounting for around a tenth of total development spending in the region.[25] But Wellington is concerned about increasing strategic rivalry between the great powers, as well as growing Chinese influence.[26] As part of the Reset, New Zealand will increase overseas development funding to $714 million over four years, which represents a 30 percent increase from pre-2018 levels, and has called for the United States to step up

---

[23] Winston Peters, "Shifting the Dial," speech at the Lowy Institute, Sydney, Australia, March 1, 2018a.

[24] "Pacific," undated.

[25] Stacey Kirk, "Budget 2018: 'Pacific Reset' Will Increase Foreign Affairs Funding to $1b Over Four Years," *Stuff,* May 8, 2018.

[26] Rob Zaagman, "Oceania: New Zealand's Foreign Policy Dilemmas," *Clingendael Spectator,* September 19, 2018.

activities in Oceania.[27] According to New Zealand's latest Defense Policy Statement, "China is enhancing its influence in the region, including through development assistance and support for economic engagement."[28]

New Zealand's Activities and Interests in the Freely Associated States

New Zealand's bilateral ties with the FAS are centered on such common interests as security, fisheries management, development, climate change, and regional trade.[29] Wellington works with the FAS through its membership in the PIF, and it supports these countries through the North Pacific Development Fund (NPDF), which is administered by the Consulate-General in Hawaii.[30] The NPDF enables New Zealand to support activities that contribute to the economic development of these countries—for example, by enhancing gender equality and increasing the participation of women in development, or providing assistance to those disadvantaged in the community.[31] Like Australia, New Zealand has also announced plans to increase its diplomatic presence in the Pacific Islands.

Taiwan

Home to six of Taiwan's 17 remaining diplomatic allies, Oceania is a key arena of competition between Beijing and Taipei as the two capitals seek to gain or maintain diplomatic recognition, in part by

---

[27] Peters, 2018a. See also Winston Peters, "Pacific Partnerships," speech given at Georgetown University, Washington, D.C., December 15, 2018b.

[28] New Zealand Government, *Strategic Defence Policy Statement 2018*, 2018.

[29] "Palau," New Zealand Foreign Affairs & Trade, webpage, undated; "Marshall Islands," New Zealand Foreign Affairs and Trade, webpage, undated; and "Federated States of Micronesia," New Zealand Foreign Affairs and Trade, webpage, undated.

[30] New Zealand does not maintain an embassy in the FAS. Instead, its Consulate-General in Hawaii represents New Zealand in the FAS.

[31] "North Pacific Development Fund," undated.

offering large aid and investment packages. Over the past two years, Beijing has succeeded in establishing links with five of Taipei's previous diplomatic allies, leaving Taipei with only 17 countries still recognizing Taiwan. Most of these are small or developing nations in the Pacific, Latin America, and the Caribbean. The RMI and Palau are two of the six remaining Pacific states that recognize Taipei. While both Taipei and Beijing provide investments to expand their commercial, economic, and political footprints in the region, some analysts are concerned that Beijing could leverage these links to increase its influence more broadly.[32] Taipei works to offset this influence by cultivating people-to-people relationships and focusing on areas of development where its smaller contributions can still carry clout, such as agriculture, health and industry.[33]

Taiwanese Activities and Interests in the Broader Oceania Region

After some years of implicit agreement by China and Taiwan to maintain the status quo in terms of diplomatic ties, the decision during the past two years by five non–Pacific nations to recognize China suggests that there is renewed and reinvigorated competition for recognition in the Pacific.[34] Taiwan's response has been to intensify its outreach efforts through high-level visits by government officials to the six Pacific countries with which it maintains relations. Taiwan is concurrently strengthening linkages through such measures as a visa-free entry agreement for RMI citizens, with similar agreements possible for its allies in the near future. It has also attempted to gain support within the region by demonstrating greater inclusiveness than China in

---

[32] Dean Cheng, "Countering Chinese Inroads into Micronesia," Heritage Foundation, October 27, 2016.

[33] Nguyen and Pryke, 2018.

[34] China's recent successful diplomatic efforts to secure recognition have included agreements with Burkina Faso, the Dominican Republic, Sao Tome and Principe, Panama, and El Salvador.

education and training programs that allow individuals from all Pacific island developing states to participate.[35]

The rising tensions between Taiwan and China were evident during the September 2018 PIF meeting in Nauru. The Chinese delegation, due to the host's recognition of Taiwan, encountered difficulty in obtaining visas to join in the Partners' Dialogue. After arriving in Nauru, a minor diplomatic incident ensued when the leader of China's delegation was not granted an opportunity to address the meeting by the Forum Chair, because Nauru indicated that dialogue partners could address leaders only when represented at the cabinet or ministerial level.[36] China's frustration at such events is likely to persist, so long as there are Pacific Island states recognizing Taipei over Beijing. However, the declaration following the Micronesian President's Summit in February 2019 called for the PIF to demonstrate a greater degree of "hospitality" to China and Taiwan, suggesting that Pacific island countries, including the FAS, may be more accommodating of Chinese interests in the future.[37]

Taiwanese Activities and Interests in the Freely Associated States

In recent years, Taiwan has pursued a variety of activities with Palau and the RMI. Taiwan has stressed its ability to provide high-quality, specialized medical care through periodic in-country clinics in Palau and the RMI, as well as offering educational programs in Taipei. The I-Shou School of Medicine for International Students was established in 2013 as part of Taiwan's goal to increase local medical capacities among its diplomatic allies. Three Marshallese students have received medical degrees through this program, with two others nearing graduation as of October 2018. There are presently 25 RMI students pursuing degrees at universities in Taiwan. In addition, the Taiwanese

---

[35] This is seen, for example, in the scholarship program funded through the Pacific Islands Forum and the East-West Center's Taiwan-funded leadership training program.

[36] "Chinese Envoy Blasts Nauru over Forum Spat," *Radio New Zealand*, September 10, 2018.

[37] 19th Micronesian Presidents' Summit, "Palau Demul Communique," February 20–21, 2019.

government encourages its own hospitals develop sister-hospital relations within the FAS. In Palau, for example, Taiwan has four hospital-signing agreements with Palau's national hospital to provide resource and training. Taiwan uses discretionary funds to support many small but high-visibility projects, such as construction of outdoor multipurpose courts for sports, and installation of solar street lights.[38] In partnership with the Bank of the Marshall Islands, Taiwan underwrites a micro loan program. Since its inception in 2006, the program has issued some $4 million in loans to over 1,000 customers.[39] Taiwan also contributes to addressing food security and environmental issues in the RMI. For example, Taipei has supported Laura Farm as an experimental agriculture and aquaculture undertaking, where myriad pilot projects are tested for applicability to local atoll conditions.[40]

Relations with the United States and Taiwan are central elements of RMI foreign policy. In 1991, the RMI initially established relations with China. This changed in November 1998, when formal diplomatic ties were forged between the RMI and Taiwan, during a period when other Pacific nations such as the Kingdom of Tonga were dropping Taipei in favor of recognizing Beijing. The official communiqué noted that the two countries would promote exchanges and cooperation in the areas of fisheries, agriculture, tourism, technology, and investment.[41]

While the U.S. presence and influence in RMI is far larger than that of Taiwan, Taipei has been effective in using myriad instruments of soft power to advance its relationship with RMI since it established diplomatic ties in 1999. In most instances, Taiwan's activities complement U.S. activities in a manner that maintains amicable relations on all sides. RMI and Taiwan have frequently highlighted the historical ties between the two nations and the socioeconomic benefits associated

---

[38] "Let There Be Light at Night," *Marshall Islands Journal*, April 12, 2018.

[39] "Let There Be Light at Night," 2018.

[40] "Laura Farm's Eco-Friendly Facility," *Marshall Islands Journal*, November 9, 2017.

[41] Ministry of Foreign Affairs, Republic of China (Taiwan), "Abiding by the Principle of Equality and Reciprocity, the Governments of the Republic of China and the Republic of the Marshall Islands Have Decided to Establish Formal Diplomatic Relations from November 20, 1998," November 20, 1998.

with the relationship. Both grants and loans are included in Taiwan's RMI portfolio: For example, in 2016, the International Cooperation and Development Fund (known as Taiwan ICDF) provided a $4 million loan for a new home energy efficiency and renewable energy project to assist local residents replace the use of fossil fuels with renewable energy.[42]

Taipei also exercises soft power in Palau through cultural activities, including opera and hand puppetry. In addition, Taipei hosts an annual Asia Pacific Day, where diplomatic allies, including Palau, are invited to attend.

Japan

Japan was once a colonial occupier of today's FAS. In 1920, Japan took over Germany's colonies in the Pacific, which included Palau, the FSM, and the RMI.[43] The region became a Pacific mandate territory under the League of Nations, and Japan acted as administrator until the end of WWII. Despite this history, Japan has maintained close ties with these islands over the subsequent decades, and continues to have a strong interest in them and other Pacific Islands. From 2006 to 2013, Japan was the third-largest donor to the region, providing over $1.2 billion.[44] And in 2016, it remained the third-largest overall donor with over $180 million in aid.[45]

Japan's Activities and Interests in the Broader Oceania Region

The Pacific Islands bring together two things Japan strongly advocates for: rule of law and protection of the climate.[46] This is the source of

---

[42] Taiwan International Cooperation and Development Fund, "Loan Agreement Aims to Fight Climate Change," November 22, 2016.

[43] Embassy of Japan in the Republic of Palau, "Bilateral Relations," webpage, undated.

[44] Brant, 2015.

[45] Lowy Institute, 2018.

[46] Shinzo Abe, address at the Eighth Pacific Islands Leaders Meeting (PALM 8), Fukushima, Japan, May 19, 2018.

Japan's focus on issues important to the Pacific Islands, such as climate change adaptation strategies, building resilience to natural disasters, and strengthening states' capabilities to enforce the rule of law. Because Japan treats Pacific Island nations as equal partners, Japan is seen by many Pacific countries as a steadying influence in the region and a country that engages with them based on mutual respect.[47] The pre-eminent venue by which Japan engages these countries is the Pacific Islands Leaders Meeting (PALM), which is held every three years and brings together members of the Pacific Islands Forum.[48] First held in 1997, the purpose of the PALM is to enhance the partnership between the island countries and Japan, so that they can better address the common challenges they face.[49] Japan is also heavily engaged with each Freely Associated State.

Japan's Activities and Interests in the Freely Associated States

Even though Japan and the FSM established diplomatic relations in 1988, Japan began providing aid in 1980. Over the subsequent decades, Japan became one of the FSM's biggest donors, second only to the United States. In 2016, Japan was the FSM's fourth-largest donor, providing $5.74 million.[50] This aid is devoted to such areas as improving island infrastructure including seaports and power supply, countermeasures for noncommunicable diseases, education, public sanitation, and waste management. This commitment is growing stronger under Prime Minister Shinzō Abe, as he wants to work with the FSM in the areas of maritime security, climate change, and disaster prevention.[51] Japan's government hopes that continuing close ties will help maintain

---

[47] Colton, 2018.

[48] Beginning in 2014, Japan organizes an annual PALM meeting on the sidelines of the September UN General Assembly meetings, where leaders can discuss the status of various commitments and cooperation announced at the main PALM meetings.

[49] Ministry of Foreign Affairs of Japan, "Pacific Islands Leaders Meeting (PALM)," webpage, April 9, 2018.

[50] Lowy Institute, 2018. Australia was its third largest, at $1.89 million.

[51] Ministry of Foreign Affairs of Japan, "Japan-Federated States of Micronesia Summit Meeting," webpage, May 18, 2018.

stable operations by Japanese fishing vessels in the region, and further cooperation with the FSM in the recovery of the remains of Japanese war dead on the islands.

Bilateral ties between Japan and the RMI mirror Japan's ties with the FSM. Like the FSM, even though Japan established diplomatic relations with the RMI in 1988, Japan began providing the RMI with aid in 1980. Similarly, Japan is one of the RMI's largest donor states, second only to the United States, although the overall amount of aid to RMI is less than it gives to the FSM.[52] This aid is devoted to areas such as improvements in basic social services (i.e., health and waste management), infrastructure development, and environmental conservation. This commitment continues to the present, with Abe stating that he intends to forge closer cooperation with the RMI in the areas of maritime security, climate change, and disaster prevention.[53] And like the FSM, Japan hopes that continuing close ties with the RMI will help maintain stable operations by Japanese fishing vessels in the region and enable cooperation with the RMI in the recovery of the remains of Japanese war dead. Japan has also provided support to the RMI in response to severe droughts.

Japan's relations with Palau mirror those with the RMI and the FSM. While the two maintained good relations after the war, including Japan beginning to provide aid to Palau in 1981, they did not establish diplomatic relations until November 1994. Subsequently, bilateral relations have grown. Japan is a major aid donor to Palau. Most recently, for example, Japan in 2016 was second only to the U.S, with assistance of over $10.4 million.[54] With this money, Japan focuses on solid waste management, environmental protection measures, infrastructure improvements (i.e., electric power generation), basic education, and enhancements in medical services. Japan has also provided grants for ports and other fishing facilities as well as several major construction projects that include the Japan-Palau Friendship Bridge, the terminal building of the country's international airport, and the main roads in

---

[52] Lowy Institute, 2018.

[53] Ministry of Foreign Affairs of Japan, "Japan-Marshall Relations," webpage, 2018.

[54] Lowy Institute, 2018; Australia was its third largest, at $1.89 million.

the former capital, Koror.[55] Japan also focuses on enhancing FAS maritime security and has worked through the Nippon Foundation with all three states. For example, in early 2018, Nippon donated new 40-meter patrol boats to strengthen Palau's ability to monitor and patrol its vast EEZ.[56] Japan has also provided support to respond to disasters. This has included aid in response to typhoons, severe droughts, and a power crisis in 2012 brought on by a fire at a power plant.

Humanitarian motivations are a key factor underlying Japan's relations. There is also an element of historical ties. In addition to people of Japanese descent living on these islands, Japan's government is cognizant of its wartime actions and has worked hard to repair relations; some of these compensatory actions include apologies and various forms of aid. And as a former colonial power that fought on these islands, Japan has an interest in working with these islands to help recover the remains of Japanese war dead. Related to these efforts, in April 2015, Japanese Emperor Akihito and Empress Michiko made an official visit to Palau, where they participated in a memorial service to mourn and pay tribute to those who died in the war.[57]

Increasingly, Japan has even seen a geostrategic benefit from stronger ties with the FAS. As a seafaring nation, Japan benefits from close ties when it comes to maritime and fishing issues. Japan is the world's largest consumer of bluefin tuna, consuming roughly 80 percent of the world's annual catch.[58] Maintaining good relations with Pacific island nations helps ensure access to the surrounding waters. And, under Tokyo's Free and Open Indo-Pacific Strategy, Japan has been actively reaching out to regional countries, regardless of size, to

[55] Embassy of Japan in the Republic of Palau, undated.

[56] Nojima Tsuyoshi, "'Palau and Japan Are Like Brothers': An Interview with President Tommy Remengesau," *Nippon*, March 14, 2018; Nojima Tsuyoshi, "Japan Patrol Vessel Donation to Help Palau Counter Maritime Threats," *Nippon*, March 23, 2018.

[57] Ministry of Foreign Affairs of Japan, "Statement by Chief Cabinet Secretary on the Visit to the Republic of Palau by Their Majesties the Emperor and Empress of Japan," webpage, April 10, 2015.

[58] Anna Fifield, "Tuna-Fishing Nations Agree on Plan to Replenish Severely Depleted Pacific Bluefin Stocks," *Washington Post*, September 1, 2017.

strengthen what it views as key elements of the international order. At the 8th PALM meeting held in May 2018, the leaders focused on four agenda items, including maritime order based on the rule of law, under the theme "We are Islanders—Partnership Towards Prosperous, Free and Open Indo-Pacific."[59] Stronger ties with the Pacific Islands help Japan counter China's influence in the region, which Japan views as detrimental to key aspects of the international order.[60] Japan is also particularly interested in bolstering the intersection of maritime security and rule of law, where Japan hopes more countries will abide the current rules and norms in the maritime domain. Tokyo has set up the Japan Foundation, which is quite active in the littoral zones of the waters surrounding the FAS. Under the auspices of the Japan Foundation, the Japanese coast guard gives technical support in FAS patrol enforcement. According to interviews, Tokyo hopes to make plans to increase its maritime security (specifically through the Free and Open Indo-Pacific) in the FAS, in terms of training and resources.

Conclusion

Several countries are engaging in what appears to be increasing geostrategic competition in the broader Oceania region. The objective of this competition, and therefore the motivations for engagement, differ depending on the actor. For Australia, New Zealand, and Japan, philanthropic outreach to address stability concerns is increasingly coupled with concerns over the potential implications of China's growing regional presence. Australia and New Zealand have traditionally focused much more heavily on the South Pacific, but they view the FAS as important as well. Both countries are increasing their engage-

---

[59] Ministry of Foreign Affairs of Japan, "The Eighth Pacific Islands Leaders Meeting (PALM8) (Overview of Results)," webpage, May 19, 2018. The four agenda items included: 1) a maritime order based on the rule of law and sustainable oceans; 2) resilient and sustainable development; 3) connecting Pacific citizens; and 4) cooperation in the international area.

[60] "Japan to Emphasize Maximum Pressure, Indo-Pacific Strategy at Eight Summit with Pacific Island Nations," *Japan Times*, May 6, 2018.

ment across the region. Rather than relying on the United States to "take care" of the FAS, they are asking the United States to increase its engagement holistically across the region. For Taiwan's part, its outreach is linked to its efforts to maintain official relations with Palau and the RMI. Taipei likely further hopes that demonstrating value in these relationships will complicate Beijing's attempts to flip Taiwan's other remaining diplomatic partners in Oceania.

To the degree that aid to the FAS is one key element of national influence, it is important to point out how even as Chinese efforts have increased, the United States and its allies and partners continue to play a much larger role in the FAS in this regard. Table 4.1 provides an overview of the top donors to the FSM, the RMI, and Palau in recent years, based on data from the Lowy Institute. Nevertheless, Beijing likely seeks to increase its economic assistance to the FAS in the coming years, particularly to fill the void when current Compact assistance agreements expire in FY 2023. China could also use alternative means of assistance— such as soft loans, as it has in the case of the Maldives—that could help build its influence in the region.

Table 4.1
Comparison of Top Donor Countries' and Organizations' Total Aid Spent in the Freely Associated States (2011–2018)

	United States	China	Australia	Japan	Taiwan	Multilateral Organizations
Federated States of Micronesia (FSM)	532.86	86.23	27.8	61.08		14.97 (World Bank)
Republic of the Marshall Islands (RMI)	313.6		31.23	48.9	51.99	16.7 (Asian Development Bank)
Palau	48.77		24.20	57.26	4.92	10.94 (Asian Development Bank)

SOURCE: Lowy Institute, 2018.

NOTE: All figures are in U.S. dollars.

CHAPTER FIVE

Implications

Although primarily aimed at the Indo-Pacific region more broadly, Washington's "free and open Indo-Pacific" strategy also equally applies to securing the FAS. History underscores that the FAS play a vital role in U.S. defense strategy. As demonstrated by Imperial Japan's actions during World War II, the location and expansive geographic sprawl of the FAS can clearly be a significant advantage if properly leveraged. In a worst-case scenario, if ignored or subverted, these island countries could become, as in the past, a critical strategic vulnerability in the context of U.S. security interests in the broader region.[1]

The U.S. National Security Strategy (NSS) supports keeping these large areas of ocean "free and open," and calls for sustaining favorable balances of power through strong commitments and close cooperation with allies and partners. In the section addressing the Pacific islands region, the NSS specifically states that: "working with Australia and New Zealand, we will shore up fragile partner states in the Pacific

---

[1] During his confirmation hearing in April 2018, incoming Indo-Pacific Command Commander Admiral Philip Davidson noted that China's militarization of the South China Sea will enable further strategic reach into the FAS. Admiral Davidson said that "once occupied [South China Sea islands with military forces], China will be able to extend its influence thousands of miles to the south and project power deep into Oceania." For more, see Philip Davidson, "Advance Policy Question for Admiral Philip Davidson, USN Expected Nominee for Commander, U.S. Pacific Command," questionnaire from the U.S. Senate Armed Services Committee, April 17, 2018, p. 18.

Islands region to reduce their vulnerability to economic fluctuations and natural disasters."[2]

China's engagement in the FAS, particularly through BRI, may result in such economic fluctuations for these countries if they are unable to pay back their debts. Beijing's engagement of the FAS highlights the importance it attaches to this part of the Pacific. It likely believes the FAS is a critical strategic location for U.S. power projection into Asia. Therefore, China is likely to seek ways to challenge American dominance there by floating economic incentives to the FAS in exchange for loosened ties to Washington. This will increasingly be the case if U.S.–China relations continue down a competitive and adversarial path. Regardless, Beijing views the FAS as relevant to the pursuit of its economic goals—especially through BRI—and also relevant to its efforts to persuade Taiwan's remaining diplomatic partners to switch recognition to the mainland.

Going forward, the United States and its allies and partners should consider seeking ways to further enhance their engagement with the FAS and to maintain funding to the COFA states. This will become particularly salient since, after FY 2023, the current economic support arrangements between Washington and the FSM and the RMI are set to expire. The same is true for Palau after FY 2024. There are three pillars to the Compacts: security, economic, and people-to-people. The only pillar changing in 2023 and 2024 is the economic pillar, but it is a substantial aspect and could create instability if issues that affect all of the relevant parties are not addressed. In the FSM, COFA sectoral and supplemental education grants ending in 2023 comprise 33 percent of the government's total expenditures,[3] while in the RMI, COFA sectoral and supplemental education grants ending in 2023 constitute 25 percent of the government's total expenditures.[4] If this significant reduction in U.S. budgetary support to the FSM and the RMI is matched by

---

2   The White House, *National Security Strategy for the United States of America*, Washington, D.C., December 2017, p. 47.

3   GAO, 2018, p. 20.

4   GAO, 2018, p. 22.

a reduction in government services, both social and political stability may be disrupted.

It is clear that the end of current economic assistance arrangements after FY 2023 represents a significant juncture for the FAS, the Compacts, and U.S. policymakers. This date carries the risk of diminished engagement with the FSM, the RMI, and Palau, and consequently China filling the vacuum. Or, alternatively, the United States has opportunities to bolster bilateral relations with the FAS through appropriate economic support structures and other forms of engagement. The next four years also offer a chance to examine prior development strategies—specifically to assess what has and has not been achieved since the FSM's and the RMI's declarations of nationhood in 1986, and Palau's independence in 1994—and to make adjustments accordingly. Therefore, this should serve as a catalyst for the opening of a productive new chapter in how the United States and its allies and partners engage with the FAS. Failure to do so could potentially come at the expense of the foreign policy and defense interests of the United States and its allies and partners.

References

19th Micronesian Presidents' Summit, "Palau Demul Communique," February 20–21, 2019. As of March 2, 2019:
https://www.palaugov.pw/wp-content/uploads/2019/02/2019-19th-MPS-Palau-Demul-Communique.pdf

Abe, Shinzo, address at the Eighth Pacific Islands Leaders Meeting (PALM 8), Fukushima, Japan, May 19, 2018.

Abrau, Agnes M., "Israel Sending Eye Specialists to Palau," *Palau Horizon*, November 20, 2003. As of December 12, 2018:
http://www.pireport.org/articles/2003/11/20/israel-sending-eye-specialists-palau

Australian Government, *2017 Foreign Policy White Paper*, Canberra: Department of Foreign Affairs and Trade, 2017.

Australian Government, Department of Defence, *2016 Defence White Paper*, Canberra: Commonwealth of Australia, 2016.

Australian Government, Department of Foreign Affairs and Trade, "North Pacific Aid Fact Sheet," October 2018. As of November 4, 2018:
https://dfat.gov.au/about-us/publications/Documents/
aid-fact-sheet-north-pacific.pdf

Barrington, Brook, "MFAT Annual Review 2016/17," remarks made to the Foreign Affairs, Defence and Trade Select Committee, Canberra, Australia, February 28, 2018.

Beldi, Lauren, "China's 'Tourist Ban' Leaves Palau Struggling to Fill Hotels and an Airline in Limbo," *ABC News*, August 27, 2018. As of November 4, 2018:
https://www.abc.net.au/news/2018-08-26/
china-tourist-ban-leaves-palau-tourism-in-peril/10160020

Bishop, Julie, "Australia in the Pacific," speech delivered in Fiji, August 12, 2017. As of November 4, 2018:
https://foreignminister.gov.au/speeches/Pages/2017/jb_sp_170812.aspx

Boyd, Alan, "Chinese Money Unsettles Marshallese Politics," *Asia Times*, November 14, 2018.

Brady, Anne-Marie, "China's Foreign Influence Offensive in the Pacific," *War on the Rocks*, September 29, 2017. As of July 23, 2018: https://warontherocks.com/2017/09/chinas-foreign-influence-offensive-in-the-pacific/

Brant, Philippa, "Chinese Aid in the Pacific," Lowy Institute for International Policy, February 2015. As of November 4, 2018: https://www.lowyinstitute.org/sites/default/files/chinese_aid_in_the_pacific_regional_snapshot_0.pdf

"Bush Signs $3.5 Billion Pacific Compact," *Pacific Islands Report*, December 18, 2003. As of January 22, 2019: http://www.pireport.org/articles/2003/12/18/bush-signs-35-billion-pacific-compact

Central Intelligence Agency, *World Factbook*, Washington, D.C., 2016. As of December 12, 2018: https://www.cia.gov/library/publications/the-world-factbook/

Chen Xulong [陈须隆], "The Importance and Function of the Pacific Island Countries to China's National Security [太平洋岛国对中国国家安全的重要性及作用]," China Institute of International Studies, February 6, 2015. As of October 5, 2018: http://www.ciis.org.cn/chinese/2015-02/06/content_7674145.htm

Cheng, Dean, "Countering Chinese Inroads into Micronesia," Heritage Foundation, October 27, 2016. As of November 4, 2018: https://www.heritage.org/asia/report/countering-chinese-inroads-micronesia

"China Donates Over a Quarter of a Million Dollars for New Madolenihmw Gym," *Kaselehlie Press*, November 18, 2016. As of January 22, 2019: http://www.kpress.info/index.php?option=com_content&view=article&id=449&catid=8&Itemid=103

"China Donates Solar Lights to Pohnpei Municipalities," *Kaselehlie Press*, October 23, 2017. As of January 22, 2019: http://www.kpress.info/index.php?option=com_content&view=article&id=759:china-donates-solar-lights-to-pohnpei-municipalities&catid=8&Itemid=103

"China Says It Will Help Samoa with Climate Change," *Radio New Zealand*, September 20, 2018. As of January 22, 2019: https://www.radionz.co.nz/international/pacific-news/366851/china-says-it-will-help-samoa-with-climate-change

"Chinese Envoy Blasts Nauru over Forum Spat," *Radio New Zealand*, September 10, 2018. As of November 4, 2018: https://www.radionz.co.nz/international/pacific-news/366117/chinese-envoy-blasts-nauru-over-forum-spat

"Chinese Firm Has Licenses Revoked for Illegal Sea Cucumber Harvesting,"
Pacific Islands Report, July 14, 2014. As of November 4, 2018:
http://www.pireport.org/articles/2014/07/22/
chinese-firm-has-licenses-revoked-illegal-sea-cucumber-harvesting

"Chinese Investors Plan Major Hotel in Yap," *Pacific Islands Report*, October 5,
2011. As of November 4, 2018:
http://www.pireport.org/articles/2011/10/05/
chinese-investors-plan-major-hotel-yap

Commonwealth of the Northern Mariana Islands Law Revision Commission,
"Covenant," undated. As of December 12, 2018:
http://www.cnmilaw.org/cnmicovenant.html

Colton, Greg, "Safeguarding Australia's Security Interests Through Close Pacific
Ties," Lowy Institute, April 2018. As of November 4, 2018:
https://www.lowyinstitute.org/publications/stronger-together-safeguarding-
australia-s-security-interests-through-closer-pacific-0

Concerned Yap Citizens, "Timeline: Governor Ganngiyan and His Delegation
Return Home Safely From Week-Long China Visit," website, November 13, 2015.
As of January 22, 2019:
https://concernedyapcitizens.wordpress.com/timeline/

Dateline Pacific, "Cook Islands Drives World-First NZ-China Aid Project," *Radio
New Zealand*, October 7, 2013.

———, "Marshalls President, Facing Ouster, Blames Chinese Influence," *Radio
New Zealand*, November 9, 2018.

Davidson, Philip, "Advance Policy Question for Admiral Philip Davidson, USN
Expected Nominee for Commander, U.S. Pacific Command," questionnaire from
the U.S. Senate Armed Services Committee, April 17, 2018.

Dayant, Alexandre, and Jonathan Pryke, "How Taiwan Competes with China in
the Pacific," *The Diplomat*, August 9, 2018. As of January 22, 2019:
https://thediplomat.com/2018/08/how-taiwan-competes-with-china-in-the-pacific/

Department of the Prime Minister and Cabinet, Government of Australia, *Strong
and Secure: A Strategy for Australia's National Security*, Canberra, Australia, 2013.
As of November 4, 2018:
https://trove.nla.gov.au/work/177494492?selectedversion=NBD50610351

Dziedzic, Stephen, "Tonga Called on Pacific Islands to Band Together Against
China–Then Had a Sudden Change of Heart," *Australian Broadcasting
Corporation*, August 19, 2018. As of January 31, 2019:
https://www.abc.net.au/news/2018-08-20/
tonga-prime-minister-changes-mind-on-china-loan-issue/10138068

Embassy of the Federated States of Micronesia, Public Information Office, "Official Visit to China by President Peter M. Christian," April 4, 2017. As of January 22, 2019:
http://www.fsmpio.fm/RELEASES/2017/apr_17/04_03_17.html

Embassy of Japan in the Republic of Palau, "Bilateral Relations," webpage, undated. As of November 23, 2018:
https://www.palau.emb-japan.go.jp/En/bilateral/relations.htm

Erickson, Andrew S., and Joel Wuthnow, "Barriers, Springboards and Benchmarks: China Conceptualizes the Pacific 'Island Chains,'" *China Quarterly*, No. 225, March 2016, pp. 1–22.

"Federated States of Micronesia," New Zealand Foreign Affairs and Trade, webpage, undated. As of November 4, 2018:
https://www.mfat.govt.nz/en/countries-and-regions/pacific/federated-states-of-micronesia/

Fifield, Anna, "Tuna-Fishing Nations Agree on Plan to Replenish Severely Depleted Pacific Bluefin Stocks," *Washington Post*, September 1, 2017. As of November 4, 2018:
https://www.washingtonpost.com/world/asia_pacific/tuna-fishing-nations-agree-on-plan-to-replenish-severely-depleted-bluefin-stocks/2017/09/01/7d83c314-8db0-11e7-91d5-ab4e4bb76a3a_story.html?utm_term=.36c00f046bfe

Finin, Gerard A., *Power Diplomacy at the 2011 Pacific Islands Forum*, Washington, D.C.: East-West Center, 2011.

———, "Envisioning the North Pacific Economies Post 2023," *ADB Pacific Economic Monitor: Midyear Review*, July 2013, pp. 22–26. As of January 22, 2019:
https://www.adb.org/sites/default/files/publication/30287/pacmonitor-july2013.pdf

Frizelle, Jackie, "The Tripartite Cook Islands/China New Zealand Water Project in the Cook Islands—A New Zealand Perspective," New Zealand Ministry of Foreign Affairs & Trade: Aid Programme, undated. As of November 23, 2018:
https://www.victoria.ac.nz/chinaresearchcentre/programmes-and-projects/china-symposiums/china-and-the-pacific-the-view-from-oceania/27-Pete-Zwart-The-Tripartite-China,-NZ,-Cook-Islands-A-NZ-Perspective.pdf

"FSM Receives Visit from Highest Ranked Chinese Official in FSM's History," *Kaselehlie Press*, September 18, 2017.

GAO—*See* U.S. Government Accountability Office.

Gootnick, David B., *Compact of Free Association: Implementation Activities Have Progressed, but the Marshall Islands Faces Challenges to Achieving Long-Term Compact Goals*, U.S. Government Accountability Office, Washington, D.C., July 25, 2007.

————, *Compact of Free Association: Proposed U.S. Assistance to Palau Through Fiscal Year 2024*, U.S. Government Accountability Office, Washington, D.C., September 10, 2012.

———— *Compacts of Free Association: Issues Associated with Implementation in Palau, Micronesia, and the Marshall Islands*, U.S. Government Accountability Office, Washington, D.C., April 5, 2016.

————, *Compacts of Free Association: Actions Needed for the Transition of Micronesia and the Marshall Islands to Trust Fund Income*, U.S. Government Accountability Office, Washington, D.C., May 2018.

Green, Michael J., *By More Than Providence*, New York: Columbia University Press, 2017.

Greenfield, Charlotte, and Jonathan Barrett, "Payment Due: Pacific Islands in the Red as Debts to China Mount," *Reuters*, July 30, 2018.

Harkell, Louis, "Marshall Islands Subsidiary of Chinese Firm Orders Three New Tuna Seiners for $62m," *Undercurrentnews*, July 17, 2018. As of November 23, 2018:
https://www.undercurrentnews.com/2018/07/17/marshall-islands-subsidiary-of-chinese-firm-orders-three-new-tuna-seiners-for-62m/

Harris, Walter B., "The South Sea Islands Under Japanese Mandate," *Foreign Affairs*, July 1932.

Hayward-Jones, Jenny, "The Pacific Islands Play the Field," *The Diplomat*, No. 26, January 2017. As of November 4, 2018:
https://magazine.thediplomat.com/#/issues/-KZUQc3lhZb_ptOmUZAl

Hezel, Francis, *Is That the Best You Can Do? A Tale of Two Micronesian Economies*, Honolulu, Hawaii: East-West Center, 2006.

————, *Pacific Island Nations: How Viable Are Their Economies?* Honolulu, Hawaii: East-West Center, 2012.

————, *Micronesians on the Move: Eastward and Upward Bound*, Honolulu, Hawaii: East-West Center, 2013.

————, *On Your Mark, Get Set . . . Tourism's Take-Off in Micronesia*, Honolulu, Hawaii: East-West Center, 2017.

Hurley, John, Scott Morris, and Gailyn Portelance, *Examining the Debt Implications of the Belt and Road Initiative from a Policy Perspective*, Washington, D.C.: Center for Global Development, March 2018.

International Monetary Fund, "Republic of Palau, Selected Issues," IMF Country Report No. 14/111, May 6, 2014.

Iseley, Jeter A., and Philip A. Crowl, *U.S. Marines and Amphibious Warfare*, Princeton, N.J.: Princeton University Press, 1951.

"Japan to Emphasize Maximum Pressure, Indo-Pacific Strategy at Eight Summit with Pacific Island Nations," *Japan Times*, May 6, 2018. As of November 4, 2018: https://www.japantimes.co.jp/news/2018/05/06/national/politics-diplomacy/japan-looks-team-island-nations-indo-pacific-strategy/#.W-REWJNKiUk

Jaynes, Bill, "FSM President Talks About his State Visit to China," *Kaselehlie Press*, April 20, 2017. As of January 22, 2019: http://www.kpress.info/index.php?option=com_content&view=article&id=582:fsm-president-peter-christian-talks-about-his-state-visit-to-china&catid=8&Itemid=103

———, "Visit to China by Vice President Yosiwo P. George," *Kaselehlie Press*, October 18, 2018. As of January 22, 2019: http://www.kpress.info/index.php?option=com_content&view=article&id=1107:visit-to-china-by-vice-president-yosiwo-p-george&catid=8&Itemid=103

Kirk, Stacey, "Budget 2018: 'Pacific Reset' Will Increase Foreign Affairs Funding to $1b Over Four Years," *Stuff*, May 8, 2018. As of November 4, 2018: https://www.stuff.co.nz/national/politics/103738729/budget-2018-1b-for-foreign-affairs-massive-boost-to-pacific-aid-and-a-new-embassy

Lanteigne, Marc, "Water Dragon? China, Power Shifts and Soft Balancing in the South Pacific," *Political Science*, Vol. 64, No. 1, 2012, pp. 21–38.

"Large-Scale Yap Tourism Development Halted in FSM," *Pacific Islands Report*, September 6, 2012. As of November 4, 2018: http://www.pireport.org/articles/2012/09/06/large-scale-yap-tourism-development-halted-fsm

"Laura Farm's Eco-Friendly Facility," *Marshall Islands Journal*, November 9, 2017. As of January 22, 2019: http://marshallislandsjournal.com/?p=5094

Laursen, Wendy, "Fair Game: The Competition for New Business Heats Up," *Maritime Executive*, September 24, 2017.

Lee, John, "China Hoped for a Soft Power Win at APEC, Instead Xi Jinping Left Dissatisfied," *CNN*, November 19, 2018.

Leonard, Christopher, "In the Remote Marshall Islands, Residents Dream and Save for Years for a New Life in Arkansas," *Arkansas Democrat Gazette*, January 10, 2005. As of December 12, 2018: http://showtime.arkansasonline.com/e/media/gallery/mi/articles/paradise.html#top

"Let There Be Light at Night," *Marshall Islands Journal*, April 12, 2018. As of January 22, 2019 http://marshallislandsjournal.com/?p=5644

Liang Jiarui [梁甲瑞], "The Establishment of Strategic Fulcrum Ports and the Security of Strategic Passageways in the South Pacific Region [南太平洋地区海上战略通道安全与战略支点港口的构建]," *Journal of Strategy and Decision-making* [战略决策研究], No. 2, 2017, pp. 63–101.

Lowy Institute, "Pacific Aid Map," webpage, 2018. As of November 4, 2018:
https://pacificaidmap.lowyinstitute.org/

Lum, Thomas, and Bruce Vaughn, *The Pacific Islands: Policy Issues*, Washington, D.C.: Congressional Research Service, 7-5700, February 2017. As of December 12, 2018:
https://fas.org/sgp/crs/row/R44753.pdf

Lyons, Kate, "'Palau Against China!': the Tiny Island Standing Up to a Giant," *Guardian*, September 7, 2018. As of November 4, 2018:
https://www.theguardian.com/global-development/2018/sep/08/palau-against-china-the-tiny-island-defying-the-worlds-biggest-country

Ma Feng, "Ma Feng: The South Pacific and the 21st Century Maritime Silk Road [马锋: 南太平洋与21世纪海上丝绸之路]," *Chinese Social Sciences Net*, May 23, 2017. As of October 2, 2018:
http://www.cssn.cn/jjx/jjx_gzf/201705/t20170523_3528652.shtml

"Marshall Islands," New Zealand Foreign Affairs and Trade, webpage, undated. As of November 4, 2018:
https://www.mfat.govt.nz/en/countries-and-regions/pacific/marshall-islands/

McClure, Joyce, "Yap Is Having Serious Second Thoughts About Chinese Tourism [Updated]," *Pacific Island Times*, January 26, 2018. As of January 31, 2019:
https://www.pacificislandtimes.com/single-post/2018/01/26/Yap-is-having-serious-second-thoughts-about-Chinese-tourism

Meick, Ethan, Michelle Ker, and Chan Han May, "China's Engagement in the Pacific Islands: Implications for the United States," U.S.-China Economic and Security Review Commission, June 14, 2018. As of July 23, 2018:
https://www.uscc.gov/sites/default/files/Research/China-Pacific%20Islands%20Staff%20Report.pdf

"Micronesian Challenge: A Shared Commitment to Conserve," 2012. As of December 12, 2018:
http://micronesiachallenge.org/

"Migration and Remittances Data," World Bank, November 16, 2017. As of January 31, 2019:
http://www.worldbank.org/en/topic/migrationremittancesdiasporaissues/brief/migration-remittances-data

Ministry of Foreign Affairs of Japan, "Statement by Chief Cabinet Secretary on the Visit to the Republic of Palau by Their Majesties the Emperor and Empress of Japan," April 10, 2015. As of January 22, 2019:
https://www.mofa.go.jp/press/release/press4e_000716.html

————, "Japan-Marshall Relations," webpage, 2018. As of January 22, 2019:
https://www.mofa.go.jp/region/asia-paci/marshall/index.html

————, "Pacific Islands Leaders Meeting (PALM)," webpage, April 9, 2018. As of January 22, 2019:
https://www.mofa.go.jp/region/asia-paci/palm/index.html

————, "Japan-Federated States of Micronesia Summit Meeting," webpage, May 18, 2018. As of January 22, 2019:
https://www.mofa.go.jp/a_o/ocn/fm/page3e_000860.html

————, "The Eighth Pacific Islands Leaders Meeting (PALM8) (Overview of Results)," webpage, May 19, 2018. As of January 22, 2019:
https://www.mofa.go.jp/a_o/ocn/page3e_000900.html

Ministry of Foreign Affairs, Republic of China (Taiwan), "Abiding by the Principle of Equality and Reciprocity, the Governments of the Republic of China and the Republic of the Marshall Islands Have Decided to Establish Formal Diplomatic Relations from November 20, 1998," November 20, 1998.

Mita, Takashi, "Changing Attitudes and the Two Chinas in the Republic of Palau," in T. Wesley Smith and Edward Porter (eds.), *China in Oceania: Reshaping the Pacific?* New York: Berghahn Books, 2010, pp. 179–197.

Morrison, Scott, "Australia and the Pacific: A New Chapter," address to troops at Lavarack Barracks in Townsville, Queensland, Australia, November 8, 2018. As of January 31, 2019:
https://www.pm.gov.au/media/address-australia-and-pacific-new-chapter

Mudaliar, Christopher, "Australia Outbids China to Fund Fiji Military Base," *The Interpreter*, October 4, 2018. As of November 23, 2018:
https://www.lowyinstitute.org/the-interpreter/australia-outbids-china-fund-fiji-military-base

Newsham, Grant, "Beijing's Great Game to Win Over Pacific's Small Island States," *Asia Times*, September 7, 2018. As of November 4, 2018:
http://www.atimes.com/article/beijings-great-game-to-win-over-pacifics-small-island-states/

New Zealand Government, *Strategic Defence Policy Statement 2018*, 2018. As of March 2, 2019:
http://www.nzdf.mil.nz/downloads/pdf/public-docs/2018/strategic-defence-policy-statement-2018.pdf

"North Pacific Development Fund," New Zealand Foreign Affairs and Trade, webpage, undated. As of November 4, 2018:
https://www.mfat.govt.nz/en/countries-and-regions/north-america/united-states-of-america/new-zealand-consulate-general-honolulu/north-pacific-development-fund/

Nguyen, Michael, and Jonathan Pryke, "Exploring Taiwan's Aid to the Pacific," Lowy Institute, September 25, 2018. As of November 4, 2018:
https://www.lowyinstitute.org/the-interpreter/exploring-taiwan-s-aid-pacific

Olson, Wyatt, "Space Fence on Kwajalein Will Allow Air Force to Monitor Debris, Threats," *Stars and Stripes*, April 10, 2017.

———, "U.S. to Install Radar Systems on Tiny Pacific Island Nation of Palau," *Stars and Stripes*, August 28, 2017.

Osman, Wali, *Republic of Palau Economic Report*, Honolulu, Hawaii: East-West Center, 2003. As of December 12, 2018:
https://www.eastwestcenter.org/sites/default/files/private/osmanpalaueconomicreport2003.pdf

"Pacific," New Zealand Foreign Affairs & Trade, webpage, undated. As of November 4, 2018:
https://www.mfat.govt.nz/en/countries-and-regions/pacific/

Pacific War Online Encyclopedia, "Mandates," 2012. As of December 12, 2018:
http://www.pwencycl.kgbudge.com/M/a/Mandates.htm

Pacific Women, "Pacific Women: Shaping Pacific Development," webpage, 2017. As of November 4, 2018:
https://pacificwomen.org/

"Palau," New Zealand Foreign Affairs & Trade, webpage, undated. As of November 4, 2018:
https://www.mfat.govt.nz/en/countries-and-regions/pacific/palau/

"Palau Asks US and Japan for Help After China Imposes 'Tourist Ban' Over Tiny Island's Ties with Taiwan," *South China Morning Post*, July 26, 2018.

"Palau Tourism Industry 'Suffering Greatly' from China Ban," *Radio New Zealand*, September 3, 2018.

Pasandideh, Shahryar, "Australia Launches New Pacific Patrol Boat Program," *The Diplomat*, July 1, 2014. As of January 22, 2019:
https://thediplomat.com/2014/07/australia-launches-new-pacific-patrol-boat-program/

Peters, Winston, "Shifting the Dial," speech at the Lowy Institute, Sydney, Australia, March 1, 2018a. As of November 4, 2018:
https://www.beehive.govt.nz/speech/shifting-dial

———, "Pacific Partnerships," speech given at Georgetown University, Washington, D.C., December 15, 2018b. As of January 31, 2019:
https://www.beehive.govt.nz/speech/pacific-partnerships-georgetown-address-washington-dc

"Pohnpei Governor Gives State of the State Address," *Kaselehlie Press*, March 14, 2018. As of January 22, 2019:
http://www.kpress.info/index.php?option=com_content&view=article&id=912:pohnpei-governor-gives-state-of-the-state-address&catid=8&Itemid=103

Qi Huaigao [祁怀高], "Thoughts on the Top Design of Periphery Diplomacy [关于周边外交顶层设计的思考]," *Journal of International Relations* [国际关系研究], Forum of World Economics and Politics [世界经济与政治], No. 4, 2014, pp. 12–24.

Qi Huaigao [祁怀高] and Shi Yuanhua [石源化], "China's Peripheral Security and Greater Peripheral Diplomatic Strategy [中国周边安全与大周边外交战略]," *CNKI Journal*, No. 6, 2013.

Reagan, Ronald, "Message to the Congress Transmitting Proposed Legislation to Approve the Compact of Free Association with Palau," message to the Congress of the United States, April 9, 1986.

Roth, Stanley O., "U.S. and the Freely Associated States," testimony before the House Resources Committee and the House International Relations Committee, October 1, 1998.

Russel, Daniel, "The Freely Associated States," *State Magazine*, April 2016.

Schulte, Bret, "For Pacific Islanders, Hopes and Troubles in Arkansas," *New York Times*, July 4, 2012. As of July 23, 2018:
https://www.nytimes.com/2012/07/05/us/for-marshall-islanders-hopes-and-troubles-in-arkansas.html

Secretariat of the Pacific Community, *Republic of the Marshall Islands 2011 Census Report*, Noumea, New Caledonia, 2012. As of November 4, 2018:
http://prism.spc.int/images/census_reports/Marshall_Islands_Census_2011-Full.pdf

Simoes, Alexander, "The Observatory of Economic Complexity," Massachusetts Institute of Technology, 2017. As of December 12, 2018:
https://atlas.media.mit.edu/en/

Smith, Mackenzie, "Remote Marshall Islands Atoll Plans to Become the 'Next Hong Kong,'" *Radio New Zealand*. September 21, 2018. As of November 4, 2018:
https://www.radionz.co.nz/international/pacific-news/366965/remote-marshall-islands-atoll-plans-to-become-the-next-hong-kong

Smith, Terence Wesley, and Edward Porter, eds., *China in Oceania: Reshaping the Pacific?* New York: Berghahn Books, 2010.

"Solomon's Sogavare Leads Delegation to Palau Summit," *Solomon Star*, August 31, 2006. As of December 12, 2018:
http://www.pireport.org/articles/2006/09/06/solomons-sogavare-leads-delegation-palau-summit

Stayman, Allen, *U.S. Territorial Policy: Trends and Current Challenges*, Honolulu, Hawaii: East-West Center, 2009.

Taiwan International Cooperation and Development Fund, "Loan Agreement Aims to Fight Climate Change," November 22, 2016. As of February 2, 2019: http://www.icdf.org.tw/ct.asp?xItem=39093&ctNode=29877&mp=2

Tobin, Jim, "Team FSM to Compete in 2016 Olympic Games in Rio de Janeiro," *Kaselehlie Press*, August 6, 2016. As of January 22, 2019: http://www.kpress.info/index.php?option=com_content&view=article&id=356:team-fsm-to-compete-in-2016-olympic-games-in-rio-de-janeiro&catid=9&Itemid=114

Tsuyoshi, Nojima, "Japan Patrol Vessel Donation to Help Palau Counter Maritime Threats," *Nippon*, March 23, 2018. As of November 23, 2018: https://www.nippon.com/en/features/c04802/

———, "'Palau and Japan Are Like Brothers': An Interview with President Tommy Remengesau," *Nippon*, March 14, 2018. As of November 23, 2018: https://www.nippon.com/en/features/c04801/

Turnbull, Malcolm, "Helping Our Neighbours," September 8, 2016. As of November 4, 2018: http://pmtranscripts.pmc.gov.au/release/transcript-40437

United Nations, *2017 Human Development Index*, New York: United Nations, 2018. As of December 12, 2018: http://hdr.undp.org/en/data

U.S. Code, Title 48, Section 1801, Approval of Covenant to Establish a Commonwealth of the Northern Mariana Islands, March 24, 1976.

U.S. Department of Homeland Security, "Fact Sheet: Status of Citizens of the Freely Associated States of the Federated States of Micronesia and the Republic of the Marshall Islands," November 3, 2015. As of October 26, 2018: https://www.fsmgov.org/status.pdf

———, "Fact Sheet: Status of Citizens of the Republic of Palau," October 26, 2018. As of October 26, 2018: https://www.uscis.gov/sites/default/files/USCIS/Verification/I-9%20Central/FactSheets/FactSheet-Status_of_Citizens_of_Palau.pdf

U.S. Department of the Interior, "Secretary Zinke Praises President Trump and Congress for Authorizing Palau Compact Agreement in FY 2018 NDAA," press release, December 13, 2017. As of August 22, 2018: https://www.doi.gov/news/secretary-zinke-praises-president-trump-and-congress-authorizing-palau-compact-agreement-fy

———, "Secretary Zinke Praises U.S. Congress and President Trump for Funding Palau Compact Agreement in the 2018 Omnibus Funding Bill, Provides $123 Million Through 2024," press release, March 26, 2018. As of January 22, 2019: https://www.doi.gov/oia/secretary-zinke-praises-president-trump-and-congress-authorizing-palau-compact-agreement-fy-2018

U.S. Department of State, map provided to the RAND Corporation, undated.

———, *Compact of Free Association: Agreement between the United States of America and the Marshall Islands, Amending the Agreement of June 25, 1983*, Majuro, Marshall Islands, April 30, 2003a.

———, *Compact of Free Association, Military Use and Operating Rights, Agreement between the United States of America and the Marshall Islands*, Majuro, Marshall Islands, April 30, 2003b.

———, "U.S. Relations with Marshall Islands," July 5, 2018. As of February 2, 2019: https://www.state.gov/r/pa/ei/bgn/26551.htm

———, "United States and Palau Sign Agreement to Amend the Compact Review Agreement," September 19, 2018. As of January 31, 2019: https://www.state.gov/r/pa/prs/ps/2018/09/286040.htm

U.S. Embassy in the Marshall Islands, "The Legacy of U.S. Nuclear Testing and Radiation Exposure in the Marshall Islands," webpage, September 15, 2012. As of January 22, 2019: https://mh.usembassy.gov/the-legacy-of-u-s-nuclear-testing-and-radiation-exposure-in-the-marshall-islands/

U.S. Government Accountability Office, "Compact of Free Association: Palau's Use of and Accountability for U.S. Assistance and Prospects for Economic Self-Sufficiency," Washington, D.C., June 2008.

———, "Micronesia and the Marshall Islands Continue to Face Challenges Measuring Progress and Ensuring Accountability," Report to the Committee on Energy and Natural Resources, U.S. Senate, September 2013.

———, "Actions Needed to Prepare for the Transition of Micronesia and the Marshall Islands to Trust Fund Income," report to the Chairman, Committee on Energy and Natural Resources, U.S. Senate, May 2018.

Villahermosa, Cherrie Anne E., "CNMI Bill Would Fulfill Commitment to Micronesian Challenge," Pacific Islands Development Program, East-West Center, December 3, 2015. As of December 12, 2018: http://www.pireport.org/articles/2015/12/03/cnmi-bill-would-fulfill-commitment-micronesian-challenge

Wallis, Joanne, "Is China Changing the 'Rules' in the Pacific Islands?" *The Strategist*, Australian Strategic Policy Institute, April 11, 2018. As of July 23, 2018: https://www.aspistrategist.org.au/china-changing-rules-pacific-islands/

Wee, Vincent, "China Renews Port Dues Discounts for Liberia Flag Vessels," *Seatrade Maritime News*, September 10, 2018.

The White House, *National Security Strategy for the United States of America*, Washington, D.C., December 2017.

Whiting, Natalie, "Joint Australian-U.S. Naval Base on Manus Island a 'Significant Pushback' Against China's Pacific Ambitions," *Australian Broadcasting Corporation*, November 18, 2018.

Wroe, David, "China Eyes Vanuatu Military Base in Plan with Global Ramifications," *Sydney Morning Herald*, April 9, 2018. As of November 4, 2018: https://www.smh.com.au/politics/federal/china-eyes-vanuatu-military-base-in-plan-with-global-ramifications-20180409-p4z8j9.html

"Xi Jinping Holds Talks with New Zealand Prime Minister John Key," *Xinhua*, November 20, 2014. As of October 5, 2018: http://www.xinhuanet.com/politics/2014-11/20/c_1113336022.htm

Xing Ruili [邢瑞利], "Progress, Challenges, and Responses of the 'Belt and Road Initiative' in the South Pacific ["一带一路" 倡议在南太平洋地区的进展、挑战及应对]," *Journal of Boundary and Ocean Studies* [边界与海洋研究], No. 3, 2018, pp. 92-107.

Xu Xiujun [徐秀军], "The Diplomatic Strategy of China to Develop the Relations with the South Pacific Region [中国发展南太平洋地区关系的外交战略]," *Pacific Journal* [太平洋学报], Vol. 22, No. 11, November 2014, pp. 16–25.

Yang Jiechi, "Deepen Mutual Trust, Strengthen Docking, and Build a 21st Century Maritime Silk Road," speech delivered at the Boao Forum for Asia, Bo'ao, China, March 29, 2015. As of October 5, 2018: https://www.fmprc.gov.cn/web/ziliao_674904/zyjh_674906/t1249710.shml

Yu Chang Sen, "The Pacific Islands in Chinese Geo-Strategic Thinking," presented at China and the Pacific: The View from Oceania, National University of Samoa, February 25–27, 2015.

Zaagman, Rob, "Oceania: New Zealand's Foreign Policy Dilemmas," *Clingendael Spectator*, September 19, 2018. As of November 4, 2018: https://spectator.clingendael.org/en/publication/oceania-new-zealands-foreign-policy-dilemmas#

Zhang Ying [张颖], "China's Strategic Choice in the South Pacific: Perspectives, Motivations and Paths [中国在南太平洋地区的战略选择:视角、动因与路径]," *Contemporary World and Socialism*, No. 6, 2016, pp. 131–139.

Zotomayor, Lexi Villegas, "Mega-Casino Resort Project Reportedly 'Still on the Table' in Yap," *Pacific Islands Report*, June 5, 2014. As of January 22, 2019: http://www.pireport.org/articles/2014/06/05/mega-casino-resort-project-reportedly-%E2%80%98still-table%E2%80%99-yap